WITH *these* RINGS

WITH *these* RINGS

DISCOVER THE *3* JOURNEYS WITHIN MARRIAGE...
AND CREATE A RELATIONSHIP THAT WORKS
- FOR LIFE

STEPHEN W. FRUEH, M.DIV, PHD

Published by Advantage, Charleston, South Carolina.
Member of Advantage Media Group.

ADVANTAGE is a registered trademark and the
Advantage colophon is a trademark of Advantage Media Group, Inc.

Printed in the United States of America

ISBN: 978-1-59932-038-0
Library of Congress Control Number: 2007923431

CONTENTS

INTRODUCTION

My mother lived in the past: she "should have married Gus" and in the future: "someday I'll be with Jesus." What she was unable to do was to live in the present with my father and celebrate her life with him.

Today I would call their marriage a **marginal marriage.** There are many marriages just like theirs. Most fall beneath our radar screens since they are neither divorcing nor are they facing any dramatic challenges.

Nevertheless marginal marriages are the pipeline for divorce and divorce is a legitimate social concern of our time. This book is written to offer a new way to think about marriage. We're not so naive to think it's an end statement. We offer it because our own marriage went from stumbling around in the dark to a working partnership with considerable intimacy and a great deal of joy. We'll share our story with you.

The concepts we present will help you to re-imagine and re-create your own marriage. Additionally we invite those of you who are interested into a dialogue. Our website is meant to be a portal of information, resources, and coaching.

My parents never divorced, had no obvious addictions, didn't drink, smoke, or use crude language. They were, by anyone's standards, good people. We were poor and we moved around a lot. My father worked as a milkman, welder, farmer's helper, factory hand. He worked so hard that he virtually wore out his hips and knees by the time he was in his mid-fifties. The joints he didn't wear out succumbed to arthritis.

They were married for fifty years. I cannot recall my mother ever expressing joy when my father came home nor can I remember him ever talking about his love for her. I never saw them have real conflict either. The closest to conflict they'd come would be silent withdrawal.

Though divorce was never an option, in retrospect it looked to me like "marriage embraced" wasn't either.

My first marriage was hormone and duty driven, clad as it was in ignorance and longing for happiness and based on an almost total lack of awareness of what it would take to pull off a successful marriage.

Hormones invade a young man's heart when he first realizes he has a hidden capacity to love and to love powerfully. The chemical onslaught is magical and turns ordinary events like the way a young woman smiles or brushes her hair into momentous occasions for self-reflection. Hormones enchant, captivate, and drive his focus until his logical faculties are dangerously compromised.

For those of us born before the social upheavals of the sixties, hormones plus duty combined to seduce us into relational agreements that were not always the smartest thing to do. We married because we should or because we had already physically committed ourselves. Many of us didn't give ourselves the option of changing our minds before marriage and so did a kind of "duty dance" that led us to the altar.

When my first marriage failed because of relational incompetence I 'rebounded.' I tried to ease my pain by marrying an illusion – that marriage quickly ended also. Rebounds are simply ungrounded relationships based not on thoughtful and considered choice, but on the emptiness and directionless sense that comes with being lost. My divorce was a shock to me. I can't say I had any idea of what I was doing in the marriage.

I was my parent's youngest son (two older brothers, one older sister) and because I had known the pain and trauma of divorce twice by the time I was forty-five years old, I became the "the identified patient" of the family.

I soon saw that divorce was not a pathway to liberation or a stage on the way to self-realization. Divorce dissolved a promise I didn't know how to keep. And even if I had known how to keep it, I was unaware of the many ways I sabotaged relationships and so made it impossible for a woman to live with me. I was, you might say, relationally challenged.

This book is my attempt to begin a conversation with you, the reader, about marriage. Perhaps you experience distance, coldness, and frustration in your relationship. You might be considering divorce or you might be considering marriage. Your relationship may be on auto pilot – not bad, but not singing in the rain either.

For the past few decades now I have become a serious student of marriage. My wife and I have created a relationship together that works. We have isolated the competencies relating to good marriages, have spelled out a philosophy of marriage that holds even in the darkest of times, and have found the cure for questioning one's choice.

We offer you a new way to work with your marriage, an entire paradigm shift that builds success daily. We don't offer perfection – our marriage is our ongoing work of art – but we do offer tools, skills and strategies that will build competencies in your marriage and give it a whole new lease on life. We believe marriages are meant to grow, to pause, to reflect, challenge, and grow some more. We also believe that marriage can be the most profoundly satisfying event/ relationship in your life. It's up to you to claim it.

Throughout this book I'll tell you our story as it relates to the creation of the ***With These Rings*** marriage paradigm. The paradigm is not a theory created in an ivory tower. It is a blood, sweat and tears creation and we look for it to get better as you, the reader, give us your insights, stories, and experiences. (Go to www.withtheserings.com for instructions on how to do this.)

My wife and I have been married for seventeen years and on our journey together for twenty-three years. We've lived in this wonderful house – a retreat where we also work – for all of those seventeen years, raising our children, parenting each other's children, and being blessed eight years ago with a daughter from this marriage.

Both of us know the pain and anguish of divorce. Neither of us knew how to begin anew and succeed. But begin we did, and we worked hard to put the model that worked for us into words for you. Now we'll share the ideas, the process, and the excitement that combined to create a lifelong journey in marriage filled with enthusiasm, joyful conflict, and tender intimacy. We created the model because we had to. We share it with you because we want to and hope it will inspire you to fully embrace the potential in your own marriage.

HOW WE WORK

My wife is a marriage counselor. I'm a leadership coach. I work both with business executives and executive teams and with couples, teaching leadership competencies and personal effectiveness skills. Together we've worked with hundreds of couples individually and in seminars and workshops helping them to gain a new grasp on the potential within their marriage. We've seen couples who didn't know their marriage could be healthy, couples who had given up, couples who had few competencies (skills and tools) for intimate relating, and couples who were doing well and wanted more.

We've worked with them, taught them a new way to look at and relate to it all, coached them in necessary skills, and provided support while they crafted a new vision together for their lives.

Most of all, we've joined with them in the recovery of the enthusiasm they had for each other when they first made the decision to marry. We invite you to give your marriage every possible chance to succeed and ask that you approach the ideas presented here with an open mind.

Although our communication skills aren't as compelling as we'd like them to be, we ask your indulgence and for you to stay with our intention so that together we create more viable marriages, and in doing so make the world a safer place for children and a livelier place in which to live.

PART I

FOR THE MOST PART, MARRIAGE IN TODAY'S WORLD IS NOT FULLY EMBRACED

Individual potential has been a subject of talk shows, books, and seminars for some time now. "Be all that you can be" is a mantra for many, and is a good one. However, relationships haven't always benefited from a call for self-realization.

This is so not because relationship excellence is necessarily opposed to self-realization but because *relationship excellence hasn't found a way to take individual potential fully into its bosom.* Focusing on individual potential when the individuals are working within a marriage model that does not allow for true individual expression is a little like putting a wild mustang in the circus. You may see the animal's passion, but to see what she is truly capable of she'll have to return to the prairies and hills from whence she came. We need a paradigm that welcomes true individual expression while holding both individuals in a 'container' that sustains their love and commitment. It's a big order.

Marriage as we know it barely works. More than half fail. Many are borderline functional. A very few are models of success in spite of the model they live within. Currently marriage is closer to a model of getting by than it is to getting high on the potential of marriage.

We will not go into the dreary statistics except for this: somewhere around half of all marriages never make it past six or seven years. Second marriages seem to fare little better. Midwest marriages fail at about the same rate as those on the coasts, and older marriages are failing at an increased rate.

The costs of heroically raising children in single parent homes are reflected in off-the-scale recurrences of teenage pregnancies, teenage drug and alcohol abuse, and a disproportionate representation of time spent in counselors' offices.

Above all, divorce costs the children heavily.

If divorce simply corrected a bad choice and couples went on to create vibrant healthy families it might be more tolerable. But that's not the case. What we see is this: most of us simply repeat our lack of understanding and skill with a new person and the children are no safer or better cared for than they were in the first place.

We've met many **marginal marriages**. We've talked to countless couples who no longer make love, or who say lovemaking – whether intimate talk, sharing, or coming together physically – is not that interesting anymore.

We know couples who drown the distance between them in television addiction, couples who are psychologically, emotionally, or physically abusive. We've worked with couples who have given up, given in, or given out.

There are couples who, while not divorced, live in a married "no man's land" where every day looks a lot like yesterday. Their marriages are held together "for the kids," because they can't afford to live separately, or because their community (parents, church, neighbors) would think less of them.

If you know what a bell-shaped curve is, we'd guess that a study of marriages nationally would look something like this: ten to fifteen percent are beyond intervention and are divorces waiting to happen; seventy percent are marginal marriages; and ten to fifteen percent are good, healthy, and strong marriages. This last group, by the way, could be mentors for the rest of us, but sadly few have been asked or been given the opportunity to do so.

The marriage model we live within today is a paradigm built over the last several hundred years with little thought given to restructuring even though virtually every other social measure of how we live has changed. The paradigm we use is fast becoming irrelevant but that doesn't mean the hopes and images we all carry for our lives together as married partners are irrelevant. We need all the possibilities that healthy marriages can bring to our children, our extended families, our communities and our world.

We simply need a new way to imagine marriage. We need a paradigm that can account for fully realized individual potential within a fully realized marriage partnership.

A. MARRIAGE AND PARADIGMS

1. *What is a paradigm?*

If I tell you that the warming of the earth is due to naturally recurring climatic cycles, I am offering an explanation of rising temperatures based on a model of how things work in that domain. I *believe* that my model adequately explains reality and can account for or explain whatever challenges you may offer.

If, on the other hand, you tell me that the gradual rise in temperatures around the world is due to increased amounts of carbon dioxide produced by the burning of fossil fuels, you are offering a distinctly different model of how things work. Yours may not contest mine but will add a point of view beyond what my model offers.

These two methods of explaining troubling phenomena are called *paradigms*.

Paradigms help us efficiently process complex data. They offer a structure by which we understand and explain events and ideas that may seem unrelated. Capitalism is a paradigm. So is Communism. Sending your children to college is based on a paradigm of how things work in this world.

A number of years ago at a large meeting of Swiss watch making families in Switzerland, the idea of electronic watches was introduced and was largely rejected by the group. Watches have springs and gears and the Swiss were the best in the world at making them. They had a paradigm that all believed in. The rejection of this new idea – a paradigm based on advances in technology – effectively shut down much of the Swiss watch making business. Within a few years Japan was a player in this game and Swiss profits had dramatically diminished.

Seeing the paradigm you are living within is not easy. I recently observed a father of a small boy lecturing his son about not hitting others. A few minutes later the boy hit another three-year-old boy.

The father jumped from his seat and in a loud voice said "Mark! I told you not to hit!" With that, he whacked Mark on the bottom with his hand.

He had no clue that his paradigm – children are to be physically punished for undesirable behavior – was in conflict with his teaching and was in fact creating the same paradigm in his son. His son would believe his father's behavior more easily than he would his father's words.

2. *A paradigm that is no longer adequate*

In the early years of our relationship, my love for my wife often sounded like this: "Let's get married." She'd look at me kind of quizzically, not judging, but not enthusiastic either. As we talked about it we'd soon come around to this: What does marriage *add* to a relationship that we're already enjoying. Our old way of relating to whatever it was we meant by marriage failed. Was it smart to try that model of relating again?

Our paradigm of the way marriage works is more about the past than it is the present. The twelfth century notion of knighthood and romantic idealism helped people transcend the limited vision their lives offered – a daily absorption in the earth with little relief – as well as give them a kind of fantasy reality to live in.

We adopted the notion of "being in love," or what a friend of mine calls "Vaseline around the lenses through which you perceive the world" – and made it a standard for measuring the quality of our lives together. Today we move a lot of commercial products using the gimmick of romance.

We are continually tempted to confuse "being in love" with loving one's partner, and the use of that romantic fantasy as a standard threatens many good marriages for it's a feeling based standard. We all know how trustworthy or not that can be. This is not to say that feelings of deep loving are not romantic, compelling, or deeply enjoyable. It is simply to notice that *as a standard,* romantic love undermines healthy, long-term relationships.

In the Middle Ages we added church sanction and the protection of property to the marriage paradigm. This served the need for stability and protection (to some degree) for women and children who were considered property. It was progress but it still didn't capture what marriage could be.

As you can readily see, these notions – the romantic standard for healthy relationships and a church enforced agreement to protect women and children – do not count for much in our time. They are inadequate to address the deepest needs we bring to our desire to partner for life.

Although protection of women and children is now 'built in' the system often fails those it is meant to protect. In divorce often the person who is best represented wins the better deal. Additionally, many marriages have little connection to the church where the ceremony was performed so that an outside observer would be confused by the presence of the officiant. The paradigm falters not because of lack of good intention, but because its premise isn't congruent.

The fourth important part of our current paradigm – after romance, church sanction, and the protection of property – is the wedding. It has evolved into an expensive party (average cost sixty thousand dollars) which gives little consideration to meaning on almost any level. Let me explain.

Weddings could be an opportunity to bring forward the best in the traditions of the two families, to identify ancestor wisdom and to ground the couple in their extended family. After all, marriage is the creation of a micro-community. This new family will take advantage of community resources and will be a contributor to the community in which they settle. Having a sense of connection and clear identity would go a long way in the support of their marriage.

The bride brings honored friends or relatives to officially support her for the ceremony. These friends rarely contribute significantly to the creation of the meaning of the event. The groom (a word that carries a history of dismissal: "a man, esp. a man of inferior station; a manservant") will not only not consult with close friends about what symbols are important to him or what of his history is relevant to the ceremony, he will more often than not reduce their role to helping the party along.

Their love, friendship and wisdom are rarely included in the ceremony or the party following. If it is, it is usually limited to a toast. What would a marriage ceremony that took friends and their contributions seriously look like? How different might the party be if thought were given to the influences and commitments of this part of community?

When I ask couples to tell me their vows, I don't get much back. Vows publicly confirm a couple's philosophy of marriage. This philosophy will tell us a lot about how this couple will work over time – whether they will commit even when the going is rough and the path dark, and whether they will relate even when they don't feel like it. (In the second book we'll take an extended look at vows and nuptials and offer some tips on how to deepen and enrich your vows.)

Will children be cared for, will they be safe, will other children in the community be blessed by this marriage? These questions could be addressed, and, arguably should be addressed in a public statement of vows and beliefs.

I believe our paradigm has become so non-compelling that we've dummied down both the ceremony and the party. Couples will receive lots of good quality counsel on practical matters like photos, invitations and food but little help with creating rich meaning for this crucial event in their lives.

B. LOOKING AT A NEW WAY TO IMAGINE MARRIAGE

1. *The With These Rings model*

To leave an old paradigm behind and create one that is true to many couples' experiences required a willingness to look foolish. After all who would think they could create a way to talk about marriage that clarified what individuals were after when they decided to marry? When I first started to work with the idea of a new paradigm for marriage, I had little sense that I would try to capture it and put it all into a book.

I did have a stream of conversations with my love, who without intentionally doing so, insisted that each new idea be clarified, challenged, and clarified some more. Like her questioning the wisdom of marrying, her reluctance drove my passion to create a new way to imagine the marriage conversation. I was often reminded of the sculptor Michelangelo who said that the sculptor released the form from the marble as opposed to creating the form. Our marble was a strong involvement with each other and a deep belief in our love. It would take work and trust to release the form our relationship would take as it will take concentrated attentiveness and effort to release your own masterpiece.

I had a pocketful of observations. I noticed that couples frequently fought over issues like money. I saw that if their money problems were resolved, they didn't necessarily move into a more harmonious way of relating. Other couples seemed chronically depressed though the outward signs of success were good.

There were couples who lived very active lives and their very busy-ness masked an underlying emptiness, and couples who indulged an addiction to television to shield themselves from their profound loneliness.

We met couples who talked about marriage as if it were a chore, a prison, or a leftover meal. Some couples were extremely good communicators. They knew what they felt and why they felt it, yet were restless in their marriages. Some simply wanted more out of life.

Few couples could articulate their philosophy of marriage. Many had lost a real working connection to their love, or the deep river of emotion that started it all in the first place.

There were couples who ran everything together so that their arguments maybe would start out centered around sex and soon other aspects of their lives would be tossed into the ring: money, schedule, compassion, parents. Their conflicts were noisy with lots of heat and little light.

To get a handle on describing unique areas of focus within relationships and to help couples see that at least some of their communication challenges stemmed from confusing one conversation with another, often believing for example that their stopping point was around money when it actually originated in fear of abandonment – we would need to separate out three 'territories' in which couples roam.

I began with the idea of three 'domains.' The **First Domain**, Roommates, concerned practical matters like money, space, and time. Roommates defines daily life as we live it, practical, here and now. A **Second Domain** shows up in the therapist's office. It is the 'who am I, really?' domain of inner work. These two influence each other immensely.

A **Third Domain**, not so obvious at first, concerned *intentional intimacy*, the sharing of deep feelings, images and thoughts. Far more subtle than either one or two, this third domain seemed to be the one they want to get to only if the life coach, therapist or counselor could reliably get them there.

The challenge with intimate relating is this: *We do not easily admit our fear of intimacy and therefore we lack competency in this domain.*

I started by calling these three *domains* because I could see that there were three distinct arenas or focal points in relationship. My wife didn't like the word "domains" because it sounded so dry and academic. In the early days I called the With These Rings project the "Three Domains in Marriage."

One day as she was going into her office to see a client, she turned to me and said "I just don't like the way that sounds."

Before she shut the door, I said "well, what's your alternative?"

"I don't know, she said over her shoulder, "how about with these rings?" And she shut the door. So, I took another look at the symbolism of rings. Rings are a symbol of continuity, trust and bonding. Kings wore crowns of gold which some said carried the radiance of the sun down through the king and out to the people. Rings are lovely and profound symbols of deep connection. ***With These Rings*** became the working title.

But we needed something more. Marriage is about continuity, trust, and bonding. It is also about discovery, risk, change, evolution. Journeys portray the idea of movement, the possibilities of revelation, exploration, and the wonderful idea of expecting the unexpected. Journeys imply adventure and that word brings a sense of the unknown.

Domains give us content and focus, but need rings for the idea of long-term involvement. Rings, holding us in a relationship, stabilize and inform journeys. Journeys add color, sound, and magic. It all adds up to the capacity for a "real time" marriage.

You'll see that there's a potential progression between life in 'domain awareness,' the deepening of commitment symbolized by rings, and the call to adventure that journeys convey. Mostly in this first volume we'll use journeys to describe the three fundamental focus points within relationship.

2. Slugging it out, or dancing in the light

Creating a new paradigm for marriage would be a dry and dull affair if it didn't change the energy couples experience in their day-to-day lives. We saw that using journeys as a metaphor for the shifting focus of our daily lives enlivened and challenged couples. To recognize where you are and to *transition* to where your partner is breathes new life into communication.

Conflict, too, benefited from domain consciousness because couples could isolate certain conversations and greatly reduce reactivity and competition between themselves. If you argue about money, for example, you can 'brainstorm' an approach to budget by restricting the conversation to the practical world of the first domain. Of course second domain issues will surface – "how important am I to you; what do you need here?" – but using domain consciousness we can agree to shelve those issues to a later time and deal with the budget demands at hand.

Competencies, added to domain awareness help couples put "teeth" into difficult conversations. Together with a serious consideration of a vision that can be shared we begin to see a pathway for transforming chronic argument into creative conflict.

We looked for the dance. We, ourselves, needed to dance. We needed to stop drying our love conversations out and instead add juice. Once we started using journeys as metaphors, added the re-introduction of our love to all conflict, and started playing with language that would lighten up the most difficult conflicts, we started to sing through the challenges. Embracing conflict became a pathway to intimacy instead of a trigger for repetitive misunderstandings.

PART II

NOT YET READY FOR PRIME TIME

This book is born from our personal discoveries. We thought it only fair to tell you a little about us so you'd have a context. It is *not* a book about us. We believe that the ideas we present are universal and applicable across age and culture differences.

In our personal relationship journey we quickly discovered that old ways of thinking about relationships didn't seem to apply. We bought into the notion that being in love, really in love, was a sound basis for marriage. But how could we know if we met that standard? After all, our former loves had been real.

We were fairly good at identifying our feelings, competent at negotiating differences, had enough individual psychotherapy to take responsibility for ourselves, and knew that the love resonating between us was real. What was missing, we both wondered, if we couldn't quite commit to a lifetime together?

Here's what happened. In the beginning, our love and enjoyment of each other was all we knew. We were immersed in the *idea* of love. We had both emerged from extraordinarily painful divorces, so we allowed the relief of understanding, of finding again how to have fun, and the physical celebration of our bodies all to enchant and distract us from the reality of our inadequate skill sets. Our skill sets, when it came to real intimate conversation, were woefully lacking.

We knew how to argue. We didn't know how to embrace conflict. We knew how to mutually diagnose each other, but we didn't know how to do the 100 % rule. We knew distance and the heat of coming together, but we didn't know how to stay in the fire of relationship together.

The enchantment of the old model – "who's to blame;" "what's your problem" – seduced us into analyzing each other and kept us from surrender. *Our 'working model' of marriage was not sufficient to guide us here.* We not only had to learn a lot about inner work and its relationship to intimacy, we also had to learn about the **Four Kinds of Intimacy**, about invitation, sacred space and sacred time. The idea of creating a **Philosophy of Marriage** hadn't occurred to us yet either, and the **Three Journeys** weren't available to help us picture this relationship. Finally, we hadn't identified the process of **Tending the Roots** and so we floundered.

A. QUESTIONS AND ANSWERS ABOUT WHAT MARRIAGE ADDS TO THE QUALITY OF A RELATIONSHIP

There seemed to be a great vacuum as we talked about how we wanted this relationship to "show up" in the world. The talk of "should we marry," the awareness of the pain of divorce, the challenge of forming a new family, the stress on the children – all came down to this: *What does marriage add to a relationship?*

If a mature couple is comfortable in their loving, and their relationship seems to work reasonably well, does marriage add value to relationship? And, if it does, how?

This notion of "added value" generated a lot of discussion, considerable conflict and some very intimate moments between us. We looked at marriage as we knew it, how we had had practiced it and related to it in the marriages of others. It seemed like a blurry concept. Marriage, an almost institutional concept, suggested more promise than could be articulated.

Some couples were in it reluctantly and would joke with us about "life sentences," etc. Others seemed resigned to a status quo kind of arrangement.

Of course there were couples who were blissfully unaware of the possibilities in their marriage and so had settled in to a kind of "comfortable shoe" life.

We noticed a great deal of masked hostility among men and women towards their partners. When we asked them to define marriage they mostly offered a tepid definition: "it's being faithful," "it's being best friends," "it's having a lot in common," etc. The hostility often showed up in their jokes.

We were faithful ourselves but not yet 'best friends.' Our arguments and lack of resolution would more often look like "suspicious friends." On the surface we had much in common but we both felt that there was more to be said, more to be revealed, if only we could break ground to a deeper level of trust. Intimate conversations were possible if we could move beyond the circularity of our conflicts.

My partner is Connecticut raised and boarding school educated. She finished all that at Sarah Lawrence. Imagine that! She lived in one house from birth till marriage. Her father an attorney, her mother a sculptress, they had material comforts, stability, and community.

I was born in Hoboken, New Jersey. I lived in seven or eight different houses or apartments before I finished eighth grade. After eighth grade I left home. I worked for and lived with a farm family in Pennsylvania for two years and quit high school after the tenth grade. From then on I worked twelve hour shifts in the factories of northern New Jersey until I returned to school at age nineteen. I had little confidence in my ability to learn or to be socially competent.

By the time my wife and I had lived in the house we currently live in for five years, I had lived longer in that one place than at any other time in my life.

This is the *first* potential added value of marriage – to create stability and community in the midst of change and growth.

Marriage is a container that holds a family in an accountable and relational contract over time.

This 'added value' has nothing to do with the mobility social scientists often refer to in our culture. Family stability is a crucial ingredient in the healthy development of children.

A *second* added value is somewhat subtler. Psychologists talk of the necessity and desirability of "individuation." What this means is you and I get to become the person we are meant to be. We'll talk about this more fully later, but the marriage container is a wonderful lab for self development, self evolution, self deepening. We could see that risking *being true to ourselves while fully in relationship* was something neither of us had ever done.

Further, marriage, a container for self-revelation and partnering, provides an impetus to self-discovery.

The first time I referred to going to a party as a "duty dance" my wife was offended. Her friends love her and wanted her there. I understood that, but it didn't interest me. I had no hostility towards her friends. I only had a clear sense that I wanted to do something very different with my evening. We worked it through. She went. I didn't. Some weeks later in a considerably lighter frame of mind she said: "I know this. I'll never have to worry if you're telling me the truth. You are clear even when I hate how clear you are."

That was a big moment for us both. In past relationships I had rarely been firm about what I needed or wanted in my life. I was the great accommodator. She was, too, and in some ways my firmness opened the door for her.

A *third added value* is a function of the second. Because we are driven to self-realization we are in deep need of its corollary, the need to discover a rich spiritual life, which is related to the need to love.

To become fully who you are you must travel the path of uncovering the resources of your own loving. *At the core of being fully the individual you are meant to be is the discovery of the love you are meant to manifest.*

Individuation – which is simply attending to the seed within that holds the promise of all you are meant to be – requires relationship and is strengthened and deepened by commitment, continuity, and relational coherence.

Relationships that hold together over time expose the quality of love in the relationship. Marriage potentially does that when you agree to let it do what it's supposed to do. To agree to continue when the path isn't clear, to stay with a partner who seems lost, to insist on your love when you can't feel it – good marriages offer this.

Here are a couple of observations that may clarify the interdependence between becoming the individual you are meant to be and the need for stability – relational, psychological, spiritual and physical – over time.

My childhood, though unfolding in a loving family, undermined my confidence in my own love. My mother was too emotionally dependent on me for me to get a sense of balance. I was either too important to her or not important at all.

Additionally, the effects of our frequent moves, the fear engendered by living in the inner city, or the resilience/ invulnerability (depending on your point of view) formed in me by having to be too competent too early left me with an artificially strong persona and a near hollow core. I knew how to be 'strong' but in relationship it showed up as an inability to be needy. And when I was needy I consumed my partner with an avalanche of demands.

Relationally, I needed to do some inner work. But I also needed a stronger, more explicit model of marriage, one which could hold me accountable and at the same time feed my hunger for discovery and my desire for a deepening intimacy.

(My partner should actually write this next part but I can't get her to do it so here it goes.) As an adopted child, she grew tough early. The combination of a New England ambience – not much "feeling" talk, stiff personal resolve, a merry social life – and her adoption at six months, together with being sent to boarding school left her with plenty of spunk, but not a whole lot of belief in the staying power of others. The ending of her first marriage only confirmed what she already believed: *She* loves but… could anyone else love her?

We stumbled along, I suggested metaphors and models that helped me conceptualize the process. She proof read them out loud. We'd stand in the kitchen and I'd barrage her with still another way to picture what marriage is or could be. I'd study her eyes, her mouth, the way she moved. Every now and then she'd say "Yes! That's right." And I'd have another piece.

We weren't yet "ready for prime time." The model hadn't fully exposed itself to us, but we were slowly breaking the enchantment and we discovered another piece that cleared the way for light to shine through.

B. OBSTACLES: GUNNY SACKS, EXPECTATIONS, AND HISTORY

My second therapist, Dan Rothstein, a Jungian scholar, was tall, serious, and kind. He liked to say that we drag gunny sacks full of our unfinished business into our living rooms, bedrooms, and kitchens.

Over the course of our lives we take our wounds, losses, betrayals, and slights, and, instead of dealing with them in the moment, we store them for future access. The importance of this idea cannot be underestimated for relationships.

It can look like this: My wife forgets that I'm working late. She fixes a wonderful dinner for our family. Time passes, the dinner cools. She's probably not thinking of how much I love her, how sensitive and kind (and hard-working!) I am. Instead she (unconsciously) reaches back into her gunny sack for a memory that seems to fit.

She grabs a night early in her dating life when a treasured young man doesn't show at all for a date they planned. He's charming about it the next day and she doesn't deal with it. She tosses it back into her largely empty sack and saves it for the night I'm late to dinner.

Although she isn't saying "you're just like him," something in her attitude feels accusing and blaming as I walk in the door. I, no more conscious than she at the moment, look into my gunny sack. There buried beneath hundreds of misunderstandings, lies an event with my first wife when I felt repeatedly accused of things that simply weren't true. Armed with this image I pull out my howitzer and fire away.

Soon a simple mistake has morphed into a serious argument and neither of us knows what happened.

Gunny sacks need frequent emptying but not on each other. Good therapists are skilled in this work and can help us lighten our loads. Gunny sacks also influence our expectations.

The bigger issue with expectations, however, is our unresolved and unexamined interactions with parents. Freud said it this way: when two people marry, six get in the bed. Our parents' marriages were templates for us. We saw what we didn't want and we also learned patterns without consciously evaluating them. Since a major portion of relational learning takes place before we're out of grade school, we come into marriage "knowing" a lot more than we realize we "know."

We begin our relationships full of hope, enthusiasm, optimism, and certainty. I don't think I've ever heard a bride or groom say, "I can't wait till the divorce." When things start to change it isn't because the one you married has changed so much as the one you married begins *to reveal who they are* underneath all the flurry and excitement of hormones. And, you do the same.

Their history and yours begins to sit down at dinner. The unresolved stuff with their own childhood shows up in their parenting skills (or lack of them). They regress to old patterns in conflict, in money management, in intimate challenges.

Many couples have described a "wall-like thing" that surprises and stuns them. They were going along pretty good and suddenly "he/ she won't talk about this." That wall is part learned expectations, part social history, and part unresolved stuff buried deep in the gunny sack.

We were no different. Although we both had worked on ourselves, this relationship and the finding of our life partner, the surrender into a deep and profound loving commitment opened us to new levels of challenge from which this book grew.

We were, and are, continually surprised by not only the searing challenges our love offers, but also the discovery of new levels of intimate talk unfolding with every encounter.

PART III

BEGINNINGS

When did your marriage start? Did it start when you fell in love? At the wedding? Or is there a critical point, a milestone, a story you tell each other that began your marriage?

Marriages usually do not begin at the wedding. Weddings are parties, and in our culture, are not necessarily connected to who the couple is. It doesn't include their gifts, their vision, their challenges, their wisdom group, or their needs. Marriages, and we see three distinct *marriages* within the one umbrella we call *marriage*, begin at surprising times. Sometimes the true beginning of a marriage happens because of conflict, the very moment we think it may be over.

It was Christmas Eve just four days shy of the eight month anniversary of our wedding. Both of us came to each other from painful divorces. We dated – if that's the word – for six-and-one-half years before summing up the courage to get married. In reality, our dating was more like two boxers circling each other in a ring – punch, jab, back pedal, punch, clench. We exhausted each other trying to discover who would blink first. Our fear and suspicion clearly won most rounds.

On the first Christmas Eve of our marriage my wife had taken over the living room. Wrapping paper, ribbons, cards, piles of presents.... her favorite Christmas tapes were playing in the background. She was happy. Christmas is one of her favorite times and she felt deeply content.

Her children lived with us. My children lived with their mother, and Christmas Eve was a gut wrenching time for me. Christmas was a time when children came early in the morning and left midday to spend Christmas dinner with their mother. No one liked this arrangement, but then no one liked the divorce.

I settled into a comfortable chair to watch her wrap presents. As she wrapped, a feeling of heaviness and depression slipped over me. I finally excused myself thinking that I needed a nap. "Be right back," I mumbled as I shuffled off to the bedroom.

I woke up around 10 o'clock on Christmas morning. Presents were opened, breakfast was finished, and everyone was enjoying the morning. I greeted my wife somewhat sheepishly, and she returned a decidedly cool kiss.

The next days were distant and polite. We moved through our relationship taking care of the roommate business efficiently, businesslike, and appropriately. All attempts at breaking into a conversation failed.

Early one morning she came out of the shower and stood in the doorway of our bedroom dripping wet, towel in hand. She said: "I think we made a mistake. I can't live like this. I think we ought to admit we just can't do it. I think we ought to divorce. Do you agree?"

As I lay in bed with my hands behind my head listening to her and marveling at her beauty, a smile was spreading across my face. I thought it was inappropriate but I couldn't stop it. A wave of energy was spreading upward through my body, warming and energizing me. Out of my mouth came these words: "No. I'm not going anywhere. Not only do I not want to divorce, I am just beginning. You see, I have found my home and my home is you." As I talked, she moved toward me. Tears were streaming down both our cheeks.

We talked of my pain during Christmas and my inability to invite her in and thus get some help with it. We talked of her fear and past wounds so that the safest thing for her to do was to prepare to be alone again.

Our marriage began that morning. We had moved our relationship a notch deeper. We had an intimate conversation unlike any we had had up to that point. Since then there have been many intimate conversations. You might say we deepen our commitment with each one. But the marriage has a beginning point, and that is a point on our compass.

Notice this. That "beginning" is a milestone we often relate to when we need a course correction. Another milestone is the roots of our love – the deep, amazing, tender, wonder when we first knew love. These two milestones anchor us. There are more for us, of course, but I want you to start thinking about the milestones in your own relationship.

PART IV

THE BREAKING OF ENCHANTMENTS

A. HITTING THE WALL OF LIMITED SELF KNOWLEDGE

If I had been able to articulate all the many dimensions of my feelings, thoughts, and images around family, Christmas, my failures, and my hopes, perhaps that first year in marriage would have been easier. But here's a suggestion that has helped me and I hope helps you:

Without the catalyst of her presence, without the force field of this love and without a new realization of the power of commitment, I wouldn't have been able to discover the power of those insights or to tell her who I was. Our marriage became the vehicle for a new level of self- revelation.

Marriages do that. At the very least, marriages are supposed to do that. *I am not who you think I am. I am not who I'd like to be for you either. I am not even who I say I am or who you hoped I'd be.* Marriage opens the possibility for discovery, mine and hers, and for revelation.

Who I am is a function of my own continuing experience and growth as well as a manifestation of my love in this relationship.

Though I am an individual, I chose you as the possible occasion for a deeper and more profound expression of my "self." I am not who you think

I am because you have within you your own version of who I am. You have created me, in a sense, and in many ways relate more to your creation of me than to the who that I am. It's my job to discover the who that I am and to reveal that to you. Marriage is built on this expectation.

B. WHO DO YOU THINK I AM?

When we met I was well dressed, clean, and rested. I took care in how I looked every time we had the opportunity to meet. Mostly I had money to spend, time to indulge, and sufficient energy to enjoy an evening or a day with you.

I shared the happier aspects of my work, drove a clean car, was interested in your stories. Your friends liked me because I wanted them to. My children were respectful of you and acknowledged our need for private evenings.

I often surprised you with small gifts and sometimes with flowers. I planned special evenings, bought tickets to plays, willingly went to your sons' soccer practice. Occasionally I would bring a big bag of grocery treats to your home. When we had dinner at my place it almost always was well planned and served beautifully.

I built expectations that, though my actions were genuine at the time, would not be sustained over time. "Who I was" was more complex than what I was able to show you. Only marriage could reveal all the dimensions of me.

Relationship is the long and delicious process of unraveling those notions and discovering, as much as it is possible to discover, the "who" that you are and who your partner is. The wall of limited self-knowledge is a relationship burden as well as a relationship opportunity.

C. YOU ARE NOT WHO I HOPED YOU'D BE

Notice this. You are not who I hoped you'd be, either. My notions of who you are may be wildly off the mark. That's because I was listening to a different radio station or tuned into a different frequency when I discovered you. I thought you matched what I was looking for but you really matched what I projected onto you. Sometimes there's only minimal correspondence between who I hoped you'd be and who you know you are.

You were a beautiful woman, mother of two small boys. You were funny, your laugh came easily. You were talented, and very eager to have time together with me. I saw you as sensitive and kind with interesting friends.

You were consistently kind to my children, understanding of my work, interested in my stories. My friends liked you. I saw few flaws.

The hormone rush is amplified when our projections are the strongest. If I create you, I will for sure love you – at least for the moment. I will believe in my creation, even adore it. But the work of discovery of who you are will lie ahead.

Soon we would both be discovering the real behind the ideal. Our love for each other would be challenged. We'd have to ask ourselves, 'is this the right person for me?'

Some couples, discovering that their partners are not who they thought they were, create a rationale for leaving the one they chose. This is often a mistake because few, if any, of us know who we chose; therefore, if we leave, will we know whom we are leaving?

D. THE GOOD NEWS

Not knowing who you chose doesn't negate the choice. We choose using personal radar that is competent in a very strange way. I believe that we choose beneath our conscious radar ("I think you are pretty, intelligent, sensitive, etc.") and that sense, the intuition of that choice, is more tuned in to what you *need* than what to you *want.*

If I need a woman of independence and personal strength, I may not fully notice these characteristics when I choose you. I may filter them out because they threaten me even though at a deep level it is precisely what I need.

You may need a man of compassion more than you need a man gifted with financial success. Your filter may prohibit you from noticing how I handle money because your radar is focusing on your need.

Choice takes place underneath much of what we consciously think. That's why it's important to honor your choice.

Honoring your choice becomes a major foundation in building a healthy marriage even when you question that choice.

E. MY PARENTS, MYSELF

I am the son of a mother and a father who taught me all they could about love, but most of what they taught they didn't know they taught. I learned about women – what they do when fathers come home late, how they handle the pressure of relating to children, their attitudes about money and scarcity, how they value or don't value differences of opinion, anger, and sorrow. I learned in my mother's emotional landscape. And most of it is not on my conscious radar screen. It shapes my perceptions, though, and when I use that filter to relate to who I think you are, I'm usually way off the mark.

I have a language for this. My mother taught it to me.
Its words are silence when confronted,
coldness when hurt, fiery attack when scared.
It was her second language. Her first was Swedish.

I once knew a woman who related to me as if she didn't know me at all. One day I said to her: "I think for you there is a guy standing next to me who looks like me and acts like me but isn't me. In fact he's invisible to me. But he's the one you relate to. I often feel that I could walk away and the two of you would still be talking."

She said I was crazy but I knew I was just becoming sane, and by identifying the projection I was no longer controlled by her opinion of me.

My father taught me, too. He had well-rehearsed ideas about women (my mother in particular) and without meaning to, I copied many of those ideas. Women would tell me that I had no idea of what they were talking about but I stayed – for centuries it seemed – in denial.

Marriage, of course, exposes these false ideas. Your comfort with self-revelation and with embracing conflict will go a long way in transforming false notions of each other into intimate conversations.

F. WHAT I THOUGHT I KNEW

I thought I knew how relationships worked. Here's a sample of that thinking:

- Women like men who respond to a challenge she's experiencing with an elaborate explanation of how things work.
- Women like men to explain how other women accomplish the same challenge.
- Women think that the best thing men can bring to a relationship is a funny joke.
- Women adore men who are housekeepers, good at budgets, and are always clean.
- Women are always interested only in a major and dramatic sexual experience.
- And this one - I'll duck my head as you read it – women aren't as loving as men or as capable of love as men.

This wasn't what I *consciously* believed. It was, however, laced throughout my attitudes, reactions, and opinions. This early learning is not dispelled in the give-and-take world of adolescent dating. It takes conscious adult effort to expose it and purposeful intention to grow the healthy attitudes that nourish, rather than undermine, the relationship. You might call this growing up.

Growing up is more than physical development of your body. It is a conscious and intentional embrace of learning who you are meant to be and of who those you love really are, together with the unlearning of most of what you've taken on from the critical influencers in your life.

What we learn and what is most powerful in the living of our lives is rarely found in school. Our task is to remove four of the six people who are in our bed. Just be sure you remove the right ones!

G. DREAMING A MARRIAGE

In addition to the baggage we drag along, the characters who have stowed away in our luggage compartments, our old attitudes, our learning, and our natural fears and uncertainties, we contend with images not of our own creation. We live in a media-saturated world where images of relationships are offered daily.

I trust you will forgive me for offering a mini harangue:

We do not interview the creators of images we experience in and through the media to see whether or not we should take them seriously. We usually view them as entertaining and sometimes "interesting." Their power has not yet been calculated, but I believe some of our enchantment comes directly from commercially driven images of relationships. That cannot be necessarily healthy or good for us.

Often in the entertainment industry, men are shamed and ridiculed, and women are given harder edges than they deserve. Marriage is a lightly held option where divorce results in hip, light-hearted challenges and children are highly adapted to their situation. It is, undoubtedly, a picture drawn by the disconnected. As entertainment it is superficial, and as learning it deceives and manipulates.

We dream our marriages and we use the imaginative material that is available to us. We need rich, abundant images of conflict, courageous images of shared intimate journeys, marriage seen as legitimate and holy to fuel our imaginations as we re-create the multiplex of marriage. More often than not we get shallow and trite, superficial and sensational. In terms of transforming your marriage you might want to turn the television off.

All of this drives the need for deep anchoring in the "who am I really" domain, the domain of inner work. It is within the ring of commitment to "know thyself" that we can descend through the layers of cultural cynicism, parental obligations and patterns, our own history of wounds and betrayals, and the goofiness that is uniquely ours.

When we are fully present with one another, all opinions, theories, hypotheses, diagnoses, analyses, criticisms, and other "distancers" are absent from our relationship.

PART V

THREE FOUNDATIONS OF MARRIAGE THAT YOU CAN TAKE TO THE BANK

A. LOVE

What started you on this journey was a mysterious, compelling, fundamentally life-changing force called love. Love is, without doubt the most powerful force in the cosmos. Some call creation itself an act of love. Certainly the children we love came from love.

We loved when we had no idea what would follow. We loved in spite of advice, common sense, or reality. Love "drove" us toward each other and we couldn't stop it; nor did we want to stop it. Love and loving feels good. It moves mountains of inertia, breaks through walls of defenses, inebriates, and can makes us as close to crazy as we human beings get.

This love quickly can get buried under routine. We can lose it when we're focused on the budget, forget it when angry, deny it when challenged. As the surge of hormones subsides we may be fooled into thinking our love has disappeared. Some people tell me that they've fallen out of love and so have decided to divorce, which, as the novelist Kurt Vonnegut remarked, was like "deciding to sell a car when the ashtray is full."

The first foundation for healthy marriage is a continuing connection to a tender and vigilant care of your love.

Love is like a child in the family whose voice is easily obscured by the noise of family life, the demands of errands and work, and the needs of bigger, louder people. By the time that child gets to a therapist's office and gets some support for what she or he has to say, they may be in deep trouble and well into their teenage years.

Love is like the flame that ancient people protected with their lives. The keeper of that fire was perhaps the most important member of the tribe. For without the fire, they would perish.

We initially see love through the chemistry of hormones. But, if allowed and nourished, love transforms into ever deeper levels of connectedness, appreciation, cherishing, and honoring. Love drives a deepening of relationship through the darkest of times and celebrates with wonder, awe, and tears the realization of intimacy between us.

Love is smart, intuitive, tenacious. We don't stop loving just because someone looks like they stopped loving us. We may try to convince ourselves that that is the case, but it's not.

Children are the standard bearers of love. They love unconditionally, they are fiercely loyal, their love is as uncomplicated as a spring rain, and love lights their faces and their work. Though it can be said that every child loves their mother and their father, it cannot be said that every parent loves their children.

Some years ago I interviewed a doctor who worked with abused children. He told me of a six-year-old girl who was hospitalized after being repeatedly hit with a baseball bat by her mother. Her shoulders were fractured as were her upper arms. She was in a cast from her waist to her neck and her arms stuck out in ninety-degree angles held up by wires attached to the bed frame.

When interviewed, this little girl didn't blame her mother nor did she hold her in any way accountable. When asked what happened, she replied, "I upset my mommy." There is no doubt her loyalty and deep love were abused as much as her body.

Believe it or not, we all share the capacity for that kind of loyalty. Our love taps into it but we can discourage, ignore, or bury it.

The first foundation of a healthy marriage is love. The challenge is to develop the means to continually reconnect with the love that got you started in the first place, and to consciously nourish it and care for it as you would a young child. It is your love and there is no replacement in marriage for it.

B. PHILOSOPHY

The second foundation of a healthy and sustainable marriage is what we call a philosophy of marriage. We have discovered that marriage is need based, and so we offer **seven need-based principles** that inform, guide, and counsel us as we move along on our shared journey.

Philosophy captures how our thinking affects how we live. A philosophy of marriage carries the idea of principles that inform and hold you when life itself can betray your vision. A philosophy of marriage can be like the two-by-fours that frame a house. You'll add a lot to it, but it's the frame that shapes and holds things together.

We noticed that the reason couples came together was that they *needed* to. They needed someone *to* love, someone who would *see* them and who they could *see.* They needed to partner with someone who would willingly *go through the changes* life offers.

We need to *communicate.* Communication is not a luxury. It is essential to what humans need and do. Further, we need to *conflict.* Need to? Yes, conflict helps us define what we believe, what's primary in our values, and identifies what is trying to emerge in our relationship. We also need *stability* even as we *need to grow, expand*, and become the individuals we are meant to be.

Finally, we need to *share ourselves intimately* with another as we descend into the garden of delight.

This philosophy of marriage is need-based and we believe that is the basis for success in a long-term relationship.

Our philosophy of marriage reminds us of why we're doing what we're doing. In our second *RealTime Marriage* book we'll take more time to spell out how these principles work and how they can help you build a strong and resilient marriage.

C. THE THREE JOURNEYS IN MARRIAGE

If you are connecting to your love and if you have created a philosophy of marriage that sustains and supports your love, you'll enjoy using the metaphor of three journeys as you explore the needs and outer limits of this love.

Of the three foundations of a healthy marriage, the idea of journeys has been the most fun to work with. We've all heard that "life is a journey." But what about this journey called marriage? Are there side trips, journeys within journeys, safaris into uncharted and wild lands?

In the ancient tale of the Greek hero Theseus, the journey to find his father reflects his spiritual and psychological journey into consciousness. After all, stories are more than just stories.

Theseus' story begins in adolescence with his awareness and need to meet the father who left when he was a baby. Raised by his grandfather and mother in what sounds like idyllic conditions, he awakens in his teens to a deep longing to know his father who at this point in the story is king of Athens.

His mother frames her response to his request to leave like this, "If you're smart enough and strong enough to retrieve the gifts left for you by your father and hidden in the forest, you're man enough to go."

Theseus is, and he does. The journey will take him along a very dangerous way – the Isthmus Road. It is a road populated by deceivers and robbers. All kinds of evil await him. His journey has begun and his first task is confrontation with evil.

Journeys, as my friend Malidoma Soma reminds us, are not walks through a retreat center or hikes in the hills above Santa Barbara. Journeys are arduous because they contain unfamiliar challenges and push us to exceed our known skills and expectations.

We've noticed that our experience with love has only partially prepared us for the dangers, fears, calamities, and surprises life offers. We use the idea of journeys to help us picture a process that can be deep, rich, and challenging. Our weddings may have promised endless bliss. Did we really think it was going to be a cakewalk?

In the domain of inner work we find ourselves irresistibly invited on a journey. Like the Greek hero Theseus, we are compelled to keep moving. Our destiny, rather than shaped by our character, becomes our character as our character becomes our fate.

It was a late fall Saturday afternoon when I rolled the family van into the driveway after a morning at the office. This was my weekend to have my four children and I was anxious to see them. As I got out of the car, my six-year-old son came running "Daddy! Can we go see the elephants?" The LA

Zoo was just 10 minutes from our Burbank home and even though the zoo closed at 5 and it was already after 4 ... I said "of course."

We all scrambled into the van and soon I was careening through the L.A. Zoo parking lot on our way to see the elephants. Parking near the gates in the half empty parking lot, I hurried everyone out of the car. We hustled through the ticket booth and were soon on our way to see the elephants.

I was striding – I'm Swiss German and we know how to march – along the asphalt paths which undulated up and down over the hilly outskirts of Griffith Park. The sun was already setting. Time was short. I increased my pace.

Looking back at my brood, I saw that they were considerably spaced and all the way in the rear was my son. He was kneeling down on the asphalt and calling to me, "Come here, Daddy, come here!"

I yelled back, "C'mon! We're going to miss the elephants!"

As he insisted, his sisters went back, one by one, to see what he was looking at. Soon my wife, an artist, was back there. My yelling changed not a thing. I insisted they come. No one moved – everyone was on their hands and knees, five bottoms pointed skyward. In utter frustration – it was almost 5 o'clock – I stormed back. "We're going to miss the elephants!" I hissed between clenched teeth.

But my son, unmoved by my sense of urgency, simply said "Daddy, look."

I looked over his shoulder and, my frustration slowly melting, I peered into the iron grate covering a low spot in the path. The afternoon sun had turned the oily water – floating popsicle sticks, plastic wrappers – a fuchsia green, with magenta circles around it spotted with purple. My son said, "Isn't it beautiful, Daddy?"

At first, I saw garbage. He saw art.

His creative imagination, connection with beauty, and his love for discovery were all part of his soul journey, to this day a journey he hasn't given up. I was clearly taken with outer world concerns, primarily time and schedule and was slow to transition to the world he invited me into.

Our relationship, the Journey into Deep Friendship, would either be fed or injured by my capacity and willingness to grow, become more conscious, and more tuned into him right at the moment it was happening.

These three journeys then are always in interplay: the **Outer Journey** of dealing with the structures and limitations of this world; the **Inner Journey** of honoring our curiosity, love and most delicate intuitions; and the **Shared Journey of Intimacy or Deep Friendship** which holds us as we discover each other.

PART VI

WHERE WE ALL BEGIN: THE OUTER JOURNEY

A. ROOMMATES

A young man I know was telling me recently about his money troubles. His car needed tires, his wife wanted to have the house painted, he needed dental work and school was beginning soon and he had to have money for his children's school clothes.

He said, "I make good money, not great money, but it should be enough for us to live. We just can't get by on my salary." The key words he used were "can't get by." He lived in an inner world of poverty and lack and had constructed a firewall between that world and the outer world of life's promise. He picked a partner who did the same. Together they reinforced each other's limiting images and daily convinced each other that it was out of their hands, beyond their skills, or simply hopeless.

Not long after he and I had that conversation, his father agreed to a loan for the purposes of paying off their credit card debt, their car, and the dental work. The idea was this: their income would be more than sufficient even with the loan repayment if they weren't paying high interest rates on their various debts. The loan the father provided was in the neighborhood of fifteen or sixteen thousand dollars.

Within three months of receiving the loan the young man and I talked again. He was in worse trouble than before. He and his partner had decided to spend some of the money on a "long overdue" vacation. They didn't pay the car off because they believed it was time to get a newer, more gas efficient model.

After living with the stress of money problems for several years they decided they "deserved" to eat out a few times in celebration of their new start. Soon, the loan money was gone but its repayment was present. Additionally they carried a larger car payment and had already added some debt to a new credit card.

The young man called because he was afraid to tell his father that he wouldn't be able to pay the note on the loan that month.

Their life as roommates reflected their inner world's fantasies and compensations, their wounds and ignorance, their incompetence still in using their relationship to create a powerful partnership.

The 'world' of money, space and time and its capacity to shape our moods, attitudes and feelings hadn't been exposed either. They had a lot of work to do.

B. CASH VALUE AND RELATIONSHIP

What this couple shared was a drama in which the unfinished (inner) business of their lives repeatedly was transformed into the language of money. When they felt impotent – he wasn't making the money either of them thought he "should" be making – they converted that uncertainty into an attempt to feel certainty by spending money. When they couldn't get their hands around the considerable responsibilities of raising children they converted their anxiety into the concrete world of purchasing objects – toys, a car, clothes. When they felt worn out from working hard, they converted their sense of exhaustion into indulgence in expensive leisure – restaurants, movies, vacations.

Money will tell you a lot about who a person is. What she values, where he's lost, their grasp of boundaries, their fantasies, and their denials. It will not tell you what to do about it, but inner work will.

Notice this: your relationship to money, space and time exposes much about you in marriage. The young man I spoke with was not able to "connect the dots" between his frustration with his career and the inadequacy he felt and his spending patterns. His partner was a young mother who was somewhat overwhelmed by the considerable demands of raising young children. Neither had an understanding that the crises they created were functions of their own psychology and their own spirituality. Instead, all they saw was that the world was a tough place.

We make many, if not most, roommate decisions in a semi-conscious state and *how* we make them points to the awareness of self we bring into a relationship.

C. TIME, THE HIDDEN LANGUAGE OF VALUES

Our decisions about the use of our time also reflect our inner agendas, blind spots, hurts, and denials. We talk to each other through our decisions about schedules, our capacity or willingness to give time to adequately listen to one another, the meaning and use of so called 'leisure' time, our choices when in each other's company about the use of that time, and the time we give to intimate conversation. All these are conversations disguised as something else.

All we do communicates. If we focus on our use of space and time, we will get a pretty clear picture of what we value and how we value each other.

Some of us notice that we "show up" differently at different times of the day. Would it help your relationship to become familiar with your own energy patterns and cycles and then take that familiarity into conversations with your partner?

A simple example of my own patterns is that between the hours of four in the afternoon and six I'm useless to go grocery shopping (I buy way too much); to engage in a complex business negotiation or to even attempt an intimate conversation. Four to six is pretty much 'peasant' time for me – mow the lawns, fix a screen, wash the car, help fold laundry. This is not so much true when I'm giving a seminar or presentation. Apparently, doing something that's irresistible to me changes the pattern.

Pay attention to yourself and time and the many ways it reflects the attitudes and feelings present in your relationship.

D. WHAT SPACE SAYS ABOUT YOUR RELATIONSHIP

Some time ago a friend of mine married. He had been a bachelor and in his early forties he found a partner he trusted and loved. I was familiar with his home when he was single, having spent many warm evenings by the fire discussing the events of our lives and was anxious to visit the home he and his wife created together.

I visited them six or seven months after they married and was surprised by what I saw. Their living room showed no trace of his life before marriage. Their bedroom was beautiful, feminine, and warm but without any of his art or furniture. The same was true of their kitchen, recreation room, and bath.

I asked what had happened to his furniture. His wife replied, "Oh it was old stuff that we didn't like that much, so we replaced everything."

"What about the art?" I asked.

This time he replied with what I thought was a bit of a sheepish smile, "It's in storage. It just didn't fit well with this home, this style."

I could remember how his inner world was so elegantly and clearly reflected in his apartment and I could not "see" him in this home at all.

Living as roommates may obscure who we really are unless we consciously bring a muscular sense of who we are into this world. Our use of space reflects inner decisions and I would venture to guess that what really happened is that my friend was not able to generate enough authority or enough awareness to stand up for living outwardly with a woman as he lived inwardly as a man.

In the labyrinth of my inner world, there are heroes waiting to be met, heroines willing to guide me, fierce challenges, and marvelous worlds to be explored.

Further, to live with vision and without fantasy in the outer world is an inner world challenge. Credit cards, reverse mortgages, and a myriad of financial deals are offered daily. They all imply that spending has no real consequences. "No payments for a year!" some shout without telling us the interest is built in and we'll be paying for it long after the product has lost its luster.

To break out of the enchantments that a material culture offers, you will need to create a clear sense of your values. What are my priorities here, now, in this family, and at this time? How are those priorities connected to my beliefs?

These questions will stimulate conversation between you. (In the second book we'll go a bit more deeply into the issues involved in living in this world. We'll look at the issues "blended families" face with money, space, and time and we'll explore how they can lead to deep friendship or open hostility.)

Remember that living as roommates is a practical matter and that its color, richness, tonality, and pleasure are all inextricably related to your own and your partner's inner journeys.

E. SELF-RIGHTEOUSNESS

We can so easily get sidetracked into thinking that all our challenges would disappear if only our partner was......

My wife and I worked at uncovering old attitudes. One that was not so evident was how often we each thought the other needed to be more insightful, more understanding, more loving... you know, more like us.

The idea that we're not who we think we are is an old one. The challenge in relationships is this: If we *assume we know* how we show up, we will be tempted to view every challenge as our partner's problem. We will develop excellent diagnostic skills and our arguments will look like self-righteous proclamations tossed back and forth like a football. We can huff and puff all we want, but the truth is that we each fully participate in every misunderstanding, every failure to communicate, every breach in intimate relating.

A relationship in which neither partner shows much interest in self exploration will look and sound a lot like courtroom. There will be an attorney for the prosecution and an attorney for the defense. There will be the presentation of evidence, rules of combat and both partners will appeal to an imaginary judge in their longing to be right.

Arguments about money often slide into this adversarial style. Competitiveness over time – who's doing more, who's responsibility is it to_____, how come you never_____? All reflect a basis in adversarial thinking. True roommate dialogue around issues of time management, time together, individual time and leisure time would look like 'brainstorming' rather than a contest.

One reason the adversarial method is so appealing to couples who are divorcing is it fits the way they've handled conflict all their married lives. It is an inefficient and ineffective method because it rarely gets to the reality of the relationship, but it does reinforce individual self-righteousness.

It may be that our self-righteousness is a protection against the many misunderstandings of childhood or it may be we simply are afraid to take a closer look at who we really are, afraid of the grief and anger stored deep within.

Some self-righteousness is born of our passion to see the world work the way we imagine it should. Some may be a misguided attempt to instruct, or teach our partner. Whatever the reason we should remember that it is a major relationship destroyer, and the sooner we can shelve it the better.

Some men can see with 20/20 clarity even a speck of dust in their friend's eye, but have great difficulty even recognizing the block of wood in their own.

F. ABOUT-FACE

The cure for self-righteousness is an honest and relentless trip inward. To do this you'll have to make a decision to take every criticism you have of your partner and look at it *as if* it's completely a statement about yourself. If you see him as selfish, look at your own selfishness. If she is insensitive, ask her how sensitive you are to her. Taking 100% responsibility for the quality of your relationship is a first step toward awakening the energies that were present the moment you chose each other.

G. DISCOVERING THE INNER JOURNEY

Looking out at the (outer) world and trying to figure out what's going on occupies most of our attention. There are bills to be paid, children to nurture and educate, careers to be managed, homes to be maintained. Naturally this focus leans towards evaluating others in relationship to our needs and responsibilities. We become skilled at judging whether or not other people are going to meet their obligations and keep their word. In a relationship, it looks like this:

We'd run out of gas. Our arguments were circular. There seemed to be no help anywhere and all we did was disagree. The air in our house was heavy with missed expectations, sour with subtle judgments. We both knew who was responsible for how awful it was going (certainly not me!), but all our past learning, diagnostics, and analytical precision seemed pointless.

We finally caved and started saying to ourselves, "Suppose this is really my creation?" I can't tell you how this came about but each of us began at about the same time to take responsibility for our own happiness. Instead of diagnosing one another, we offered, tentatively at first, inner discoveries we were facing that greatly impacted our relationship.

This subtle yet momentous shift in attitude was surprising to each of us. Like surrender to your partner's natural genius, taking 100% responsibility when you are in conflict can feel like total exposure. As if someone just pulled your mask off, only in this case, it's you that are doing the unmasking.

Because of our total focus on living in this world, we often lose an awareness of who *we* are, what *our* needs are, what *our* fears are, what desire we are tapping into in by setting certain goals, what our dreamtime stories are telling us, who we love, and even how our personal history is possibly skewing our judgments or driving our priorities.

You can discover the spine-tingling adventure of becoming aware of your own self. It takes a little work but you can do it. Facing it consciously, disclosing your discoveries to your partner in intimate conversation, and reaping the rewards of personal congruence changes the ownership of your life. Embarking on this inner journey is not only a fascinating adventure full of surprises, but your work here builds congruence between the inner and outer worlds that make up your life.

The inner journey takes you *in* and *down* to the heart of your relational consciousness, *down* into the labyrinth of soul. Behind the mysteries of addiction you will discover the meaning of losses and betrayals, and hidden around the corner from chronic argumentativeness, you'll find abandonment and serious wounds.

You'll also have the opportunity to explore rich veins of creativity and golden threads of energy laced among the hard rock of lost time. As you descend, there is spiritual resonance offering clues to the very *why* of your existence. This kind of work has no limit. Our self knowledge is touched as if by a finger that reaches in from the conscious world.

Inner work is the natural complement to the work we do in the "outer" world, our life as roommates. Without awareness of who we are or what we're really about, our daily affairs become boring, one-dimensional, and without insight. If you take a closer look at your life in the first domain some of this will become clearer.

Inner journey challenges look like the discovery of courage, integrity, and whether or not we have the capacity to love. The inner journey, seen through our lives in the outer world, will point to unnamed fears, anxieties, fantasies, and obsessions that should sound the alarm and prepare us for inner exploration.

Inner journeys expose our motives when we have lived behind carefully crafted personas. They slowly or dramatically remove the mask created so artfully over the years as a survival necessity. Our own inner journey will help us to stop wondering why we feel bad or are victimized by moods, or why we feel misunderstood.

Inner journeys are a good alternative to drugs, illegal, or prescriptive. When we begin taking 100% responsibility for the quality of our lives, when we start pulling back the projections we have plastered all over our partners, when we risk looking stupid, ignorant or lost by revealing who we really are… we are going inward towards integrity and outward toward legitimacy in the world.

The quality of that inner journey will be felt in our outer lives together. Later on we'll look at the interrelationship between one's inner life and the Journey into Intimacy. You'll need willingness, courage, and determination to open the many doors to wisdom that are there and have been there all along waiting for you to turn the key.

Theseus has a wonderful moment of insight as he's on his way to meet his father. Having conquered the road of trouble he continues on to Athens. He is met by a large crowd. Head and shoulders above the crowd the face of a beautiful woman stands out. She is the queen.

This ancient kingdom is a kingdom run by women and it relies for the abundance of its crops on fertility rights and rituals. Unknown to Theseus an annual event decides who will serve as king for the next year.

Theseus in meeting the crowd on the road is soon drawn into the festivities. In deciding to stay a while he soon realizes his fate is to wrestle the king in a death match. The winner, in this ancient fertility rite, will be king for the coming year.

Upon his success, Theseus indeed becomes king. But it's a deal few of us would want.

Here's how it worked. The daily business of the kingdom was organized and run by women. All important decisions were made by the queen. Theseus is told to "go play with the boys." He hunts, takes part in athletic contests, and plays games. This is fun at first, but it starts wearing thin. Though his nights are great, the days become boring.

One day Theseus, noticing the way "things are run around here," challenges the queen to make some changes. She simply brushes him off. He sees what he's up against. The king is needed only to satisfy the demands of the ritual. He is a 'figurehead' in every sense of the word. Facing the futility of a life in which his leadership is marginal at best he decides it's time to move on.

"I no longer can be a man by night and a boy by day," he says and he decides to leave this gilded life.

I once had a close friend who described herself as the "original pipe and slippers girl." Like Theseus, she, was taking a look at her own imprisonment in an image that once worked for her but no longer served her identity.

The amazing thing is this kind of enchantment is often blamed on one's partner. *He* made me "the original pipe and slippers girl" or *she* wouldn't let me have my authority, opinion, or point of view. Like the couple who finish each other's sentences, these folks are used to dysfunction and when consciousness comes, they find it easy to blame someone else for their lost lives.

The inner journey often begins with the breaking of an enchantment. Awakening to a self induced state of partial consciousness we notice the sun for the first time. If we can claim this brief opportunity for conscious realization of who we are and who we might be, we have a chance to open our relationship to vitality and real growth. If not, every day will look a lot like yesterday.

For more on enchantments, take another look at fairy tales. Check out Marie Louise Von Franz' *The Feminine in Fairy Tales* and Robert Bly's *Iron John* and you'll get a better sense of this.

Notice that the inner journey is basic to partnership because of this:

If you don't know who you are, how can I know whom I am loving?

PART VII

THE INNER JOURNEY

A. DESCENT

What does it mean to you if I tell you the inner journey is about descent? Descent is a word we use in this world to point a direction. It is tangible and clear. But the word descent when used in the inner world conveys leaving an outer world focus and instead attending to the imaginative world of thoughts, dreams, fantasies, and images.

We like to imagine these as lying deeper within than the stream of ideas, decisions, thoughts, and images that flow into our heads throughout the day.

Exposing the images tucked within the maze of paths and caverns of our inner world and which contain a huge percent of who we are - but which is not immediately accessible to ordinary conscious thought - will expose love we forgot we had, genius we never explored, wounds long buried, and attitudes formed ages ago.

The inner journey will expose the psychology of the 'orphan' – the one stuck at a developmental stage who is bullied by fear, the one shown to the world as indecisive, insecure, and incomplete. He or she will make deals to gain the approval of others, defer repeatedly to the force field of others, listen for applause, live in "maybe," and spend a lot of time in "if only."

Many marriages end when one of the partners awakens to the depth and pain of living a counterfeit life. It may not be necessary to end it, but fear is so powerful that they may, at that moment, be unable to see a path that is possible. We call these divorces *marriages aborted.*

In the labyrinth of my inner world, there are heroes waiting to be met, heroines willing to guide me, fierce challenges, and marvelous worlds yet unexplored.

Inner work is the work of the hero. Mythic tales capture an inner process that resonates with us. Taking on evil in whatever form clears away the debris that clouds our vision.

It is a challenge to live your own life fully, and relationships sharpen the challenge. Confronting a life that others would design for us, whether that other is our parents, our partners, or our community is a mature adult's responsibility. To be a contributing member of a community means that you have to have a tangible grasp of your own individual presence, gifts, boundaries, and love. And to do that, you have to let go of the templates others have designed for you and descend into the truth of your own *inner* reality.

To love another means you'll have to claim your own authority, the unique manifestation of your loving, your own true needs, and the clear access to Yes and to No that loving requires.

B. RESPONSIBILITY

When I (finally) was able to stop diagnosing and analyzing my partner and instead took a long hard look inward, it wasn't obvious to me exactly what I needed to do. What was obvious, though, was relief. I could feel a great weight lift from our relationship as I began, tentatively at first, to take full responsibility for my own happiness.

Inner work was not new to me. I had already spent years in psychotherapy. What was new was that my happiness, my sense of relational power, and my loving were entirely my challenge. She may surely influence how I feel, but my decisions about myself were mine to own. I decided to have faith and take 100% responsibility for my loving.

Today is not only the first day of the rest of your life,
in terms of your marriage, it's the only day.

A friend of mine, fresh out of a weekend intensive in which he focused on responsibility, said it this way, "my life works when I keep my agreements."

He meant all agreements and that meant not only taking responsibility for the agreements he made but also for the agreements he would be making or was now in the process of making. Life works, you could say, when we consciously accept that our agreements are our way of connecting with what's valuable and precious in this life.

C. WORKING WITH YOUR INNER WORLD

That same friend also liked to say this to me: "I was born at night, but it wasn't last night." I like that because it reminds me that whatever I offer in this new way of imagining marriage will not automatically translate easily into behavior change on your part. It takes work to know yourself and the humility to admit that maybe the self you know isn't as well-known as you'd like to think it is.

Most of us need a wisdom partner – a coach, a therapist, a spiritual advisor or a truly centered and conscious friend. Some can do it in partnership with their husband or wife. My advice is to start with a good coach or therapist and learn the basics of inner work. We will introduce you to some of the dimensions you may explore. Trust that you have a coherent inner self and as you begin to read, explore, and journal, good things will happen.

D. DREAMS

When I ask people about their dreams, many shrug or laugh nervously and say: "I don't remember my dreams. Does everyone dream?" We live in a culture where our imaginations, like our bodies, are under-utilized. Television, radio, and other forms of the media imagine *for* us. We "dummy down" our imaginations and reduce the range and depth of our conversations accordingly.

Loss of contact with our dreams deprives us of a rich source of information that can guide, inspire, clarify, and inform our relationships. (You may want to check out Robert Bosnak's book *A Little Course on Dreams* for some help.)

The challenge is to tune in to a different kind of information delivery system. The imagery of dreams brings meaning to us but not in the forms we're used to. That is, not in a rational, logical, sequential form.

I dreamed once of being invited to an event. It was a privilege to attend. I lived within walking distance and as I approached the destination I was amazed. For it took place in a lovely, elegant mansion situated on a grassy hill dotted with trees.

At the gate there were luxuriously dressed guards checking the credentials of what turned out to be a large crowd of people waiting to get in.

I passed in easily, my credentials not even needing to be checked. Behind me, my father and brothers also were admitted. But close friends, in-laws, and several professors I knew were denied entrance.

Once inside I was escorted by a beautiful and elegantly dressed woman into a large hall in which everything was covered in red velvet. She instructed me that I was to be the guest of honor and I would be seated on a platform toward the front of the hall. As she spoke, tables rose out of the floor covered in red velvet set with the finest silverware and extraordinary crystal.

Soon there was a banquet. Toasts and honors were given and a strange sense of transformation overcame me. I was aware of a deep sense of legitimacy such that I had never known.

Later as I wandered among the mansions' many rooms, I stopped and focused on one room. I was on my hands and knees looking for something but I didn't know what, searching the hardwood floor. Someone standing by my side said, "This is what you're looking for," and began to drop large gold coins by my side. I looked up as the coins became a pile. It was my father and he seemed to have an endless supply of gold in his pockets…

The work:

My third year of psychotherapy had been a year of incredible challenge and change. I was aware of a deep struggle for acceptance and I was working with declaring the kind of life I wanted to live. I knew that my life, in many ways, had been driven and shaped by others. The idea of being an "orphan" occurred to me at this time though it was an idea related to an inner sense of longing to belong rather than an outward situation. I hadn't yet given enough weight to the impact my relationship with my mother or father, my distance and denial – had on the depth of my aloneness. I focused on the recurrent sense I had of being an outsider, a loner, and one who was driven to impress others.

The sense that my life was shaped by others related to the many compromises made on my survival path – my own trail of tears. As I worked with my dreams and my history I opened slowly to my own deep wounds. I began sharing some of these with my family, began challenging my career choice, began confronting lies I had told myself.

In addition to this work, I started to "actively imagine" and re-experience personal milestones – painful and joyful – and in doing so moved into a deeper realization of not only who I was not, but who I was, whether or not anyone approved.

This was the endless gold my father offered me. I was on the way to realizing and accepting my own legitimacy.

Dreams will prod us, point us, unnerve us, inspire us. Whatever is happening in your dreams, it pays to take them seriously.

What does it mean if I dream that my life is a well-decorated prison? Am I gearing up for a career change? Have my inner orphan and my outer self constructed a life in which I have fewer and fewer options?

If I dream my parents' marriage was built on a poor foundation, is that dream about my parents or me?

Freud said over 100 years ago that dreams will open the door to the unconscious. They will also connect us with the community of men and women who, we discover, are more like us than strangers to us.

Dreams may be the deepest and most trustworthy source of information about who you really are. As the youth of today would say, "Dreams rock."

Early childhood learning has a lasting influence on our hopes, fears, and longing. Uncovering and recovering experiences we have forgotten or repressed opens into insights, especially those regarding chronic conflict. A political historian once said "He who forgets the past is condemned to repeat it."

I was on my way to a gathering of men some years ago. The gathering took place deep within the woods in Mendocino County. As I pulled off the blacktop and began to drive down a dirt road I increasingly became short of breath. As I drove farther down the road, the shortness of breath began to alarm me. I could hardly breathe. I pulled over.

As I sat in my car trying to recapture my natural breathing I flashed back to a time when I was eight or nine years old and was badly hurt by a man who tricked me into following him down a hill and into the woods. Now, as I drove down the road into these woods my body was remembering the wound long before "I" could retrieve it.

E. HISTORY

When people ask me why they should go back and deal with wounds and losses of their childhood – their individual history – I tell them that "you are 'dealing' with them. Your body has memory just as your brain does. It's never a question of *whether* you deal with the wounds of your childhood, it's *how* you deal with them."

I believe that we shrink from our wounds and losses because we either don't have the support or we lack the competence to do so. Good therapists are extremely valuable here because they can not only support your right to expose your wounds to the healing insights of the adult you have become, but they can also help you gain the competence and the confidence to do so.

"I've been through all of that!" She fairly screamed at me, "I don't want to go there! Why does it always have to be about the parents? I'm an adult. Can't I simply let the past be and move on!?"

This woman was attending a workshop we offered and I was talking about personal history – mine and my partner's. Her reaction and emotion soon let her know we had hit upon a mother lode. She knew she wasn't finished with the abuse she suffered growing up, but she was very afraid that there was nothing that could be done about it. The hope of gaining competency by taking on her childhood was truly life-altering.

In gaining the courage to consciously look at her own wounds, she started a new path with her husband. Instead of the villain (that he often volunteered to be) he slowly became a partner as they together transformed the monotonous patterns of distance and blame to vulnerability and sharing.

Our history walks around with us, shows up at the job, the grocery store, even in bed. It sits down with us at the kitchen table and seeps through when we begin thinking about making love. Here's more good news: we get to choose. Will our history shape our lives, our thoughts our desire to be close or will we reshape our history and let it manifest in a way that feeds and nourishes our lives and relationships?

F. GENDER

We are who we are and we are always becoming who we are. We have a stable inner sense of our femininity or masculinity, and yet we are forever discovering new dimensions of ourselves.

Years ago I was fascinated and surprised as I watched an older man who had been a mentor to me become "softer" and more observant as he aged. He seemed to morph into a more feminine man without losing any of the qualities of masculinity that I had always admired in him.

I have known women who seemed to get more linear, task-driven, and less "motherly" as they aged – aspects we would usually associate with the masculine.

Do we need less and less gender identity as we mature, or are we always learning, borrowing, and evolving in our gender definition?

Inner work brings you to themes like this: how would a true woman show up in this conversation? What does a forty-year-old man do with a fifteen-year-old son? What aspects of my identity are truly mine? What aspects have I borrowed or taken on from others? What can I discard today?

Many men I know felt very fortunate to be able to attend men's gatherings led by Robert Bly, the poet; Michael Meade, the story teller, mythologist and drummer; and James Hillman, psychologist, writer extraordinaire, and tap dancer. There were many other teachers also. These men gave a good deal of thought, time, and effort to helping men find a definition of their masculinity that would be grounded in ancestral images and contemporary in addressing the challenges we face today. The gatherings were empowering, inspirational, and full of good information. I went to many of these gatherings and was deeply moved by the depth, intelligence and commitment of men who knew they wanted to realize a deeper appreciation for the masculine. They also knew that their going there would feed and nourish the women in their lives.

Defining myself in terms of the unique attributes of my gender doesn't cancel out the many thousands of ways I am simply human, a person among persons, a Homo sapiens. It is essential that we tune into our own inner resonances, the gifts of our masculine or feminine inclinations, and the instinctive attributes we bring to family and community. Without that, we lose the unique gifts of gender distinctiveness.

It also helps to end self shaming. By shaming, I mean that without gender consciousness I may confuse my wife's gifts with deficits I carry. I may compete with her rather than learn from her. I may shut her down when I need to open up. Self shaming is learned behavior; the unlearning of shame is a big project for many men and women.

Books

There are all kinds of resources available for your exploration. For those of you who want to know more feel free to contact us through the ***With These Rings*** web site.

Men may want to check out Michael Meade's *Men and the Water of Life* as well as Bly's *Iron John*. Of course there are many others, but these are two of my favorites.

For women, I like Clarissa Pinkola Estes' *Women who Run with the Wolves,* Linda Leonard's wonderfully insightful books, and Maureen Murdock's *The Heroines Journey*. The poetry of Mary Oliver and Sharon Olds is excellent, and so is *The Rag and Bone Shop of the Heart* edited by Bly, Hillman and Meade. There are many very helpful books out there.

Begin with one of these and follow your instincts. There you will find plenty of material for beginning intimate conversations with your partner. The Journey into Intimacy has many paths. The trick is to begin.

G. SOUL MATES

The poet Rumi says our lovers aren't "out there" – they are within us all along. The soul mate we long for is an inner twin, a presence we are born with and forget. Perhaps life is simply about finding her or him, the home we thought we lost, the love that has been ours from before birth, our legitimate heritage.

Inner work depends on the exploration of images. Dreams provide rich images for you to work with; our exploration of gender awareness also is abundant in imagery. We each carry a deep longing for soul knowledge that informs our journey and challenges our assumptions.

Within the domain of inner work we may tune into a kind of resonance that confirms or cautions us in the direction we are going. This tonal quality of our inner being anchors inner truth and reflects the very vibrations of the cosmos.

Looking for your soul mate within helps you to tune into a counter intuitive sense of who you are as well as helps you withdraw the projections from the men or women you have mistakenly given them to. Your inner "soul mate" insists that you claim the fullness of your own being in all its manifestations.

We have discovered that inner work, tuning into your dream life, searching for and finding your (inner) soul mate – all of these are closely allied with your spiritual journey.

H. SPIRITUALITY

This is a much abused word. Some confuse spirituality with religion, some with orthodox (from *ortho*, "straight") thinking. Not too much of spirituality as I've come to know it is akin to a straight line. Our image is closer to a spiral.

There are those who believe spirituality concerns a socially equitable process. Others think ecstasy is the definition of spirituality. I have heard people describe a particular person as "very spiritual" and I have learned to be cautious around that person.

Spirituality is *not* about being ungrounded, falsely positive, soft spoken, or passively compliant. It is not about being zealous around a particular religious point of view, superior morally, or self-righteous. It is not a big smile.

Spirituality is about resonance with the ground of being. It is about awe when in the awareness of creation. Jesus of Nazareth was an amazing teacher. He pointed out that children (I like to think of your average four-to-six-year old) know more about spirituality than most adults. He didn't go for rules, power struggles, or exclusionary tactics. Truth, you might say, qualified as real spirituality for Jesus. And he saw truth in what you did rather than what you said.

Developing an appreciation of your own spirituality will mean you will have to know something about your loving.

Losing contact with the depth and resonance of your love
will leave you feeling and acting like an orphan.

Marriage requires a well-thought-through value system. We call it a *philosophy of marriage*. Our first principle is the need to love and the need to have your loving received.

Many people have said to me, "Don't you mean the need to *be* loved?"

I respond: "Well, it's nice to be loved. I like it. But my own spiritual presence is based on my capacity *to* love."

That capacity has been undermined in a number of ways. I was taught that the way I love wasn't appropriate, or that my love was too much, or that my anger wasn't loving, or that my sexual presence wasn't loving or that my No wasn't loving.

I had to do a fair amount of inner work to clean out the debris of this kind of education so that I could get back to a clear and resonant definition of my own love. Beyond that, I had to rediscover that I didn't create myself. I wasn't an independent, non-connected being set loose in the universe by pure chance. There was a resonance that touched me even as I was reaching to touch it. This resonance has many names, but I prefer to call this presence God.

I. INTENTION, FOCUS, AND DISCIPLINE

Working with the inner world is not simply a matter of expressing how you feel or writing down your dreams. Those are both good, but inner work works because of three words: *intention, focus, and discipline.*

Intention: I not only would *like* to become more fully who I am, but I *commit* to it. Intention is an act of will. I awaken my will in the service of an expedition. Intention invites your deepest attention to the exploration, revelation, and exposure of images, memories, experiences, feelings, thoughts, and desires which have been mostly kept out of sight.

Focus serves intention like a searchlight penetrates the darkness. I have heard it said that "you are what you focus on." Focus grabs us and rivets our attention to the subjects we wish to explore. Without focus we are tossed about, never stopping long enough to realize our identity.

Intention and focus work because of practice, which is the fruit of *discipline*. Marie Louise Von Franz, an eminent Jungian analyst and writer, once told an audience in Davos, Switzerland, that she spent one to two hours each morning working on her dreams. She took this time *before* her work day began.

Self knowledge is not about luck, genes, or brilliance. It's about a deep longing to know and to heal yourself. The competencies we reviewed above – dreams, history, gender, spirituality, soul mates – are aspects of inner work. What's important now is that you begin. Or if you've begun, that you continue to deepen your own inner work.

J. EMOTION'S LANDSCAPE

Psychotherapy has long focused on the quality, shape, and expression of emotion. Many couples have experienced growth by working with long repressed feelings, identifying and clarifying certain strong feelings such as anger or sorrow, and by learning how to listen non-judgmentally to their partner. Their work has moved them closer and made their relationships far richer.

In the *With These Rings* model we honor that work and invite couples to consider the landscape of each domain as it relates to emotional tones and needs. Naturally anxiety will be felt in the first journey because quick decisions are often called for and because the first domain isn't strong on reflection. It's an action kind of place. Anxiety can morph into anger in a "New York second," so couples will have to be vigilant about their responses to anxiety when in this domain.

Inner work and its deep emphasis on reflection stimulate the release of deep emotion. We'll be vulnerable to self shaming. We'll want to deny what we feel because we've been subject to years of suppression. Within many "inner conversations" there is also relief, the release of repressed emotion and profound joy.

The overriding emotions of the third journey may be awe, deep tenderness, wonder, and an earthy kind of resonant loving. This journey requires honoring your partner, honoring yourself, slowing down, and tuning in.

PART VII

THE JOURNEY INTO INTIMACY

A. BY INVITATION ONLY

In the outer world journey we use ordinary language. The first domain is a world of practical conversations including negotiating differences, agreements, and compromises. Its substance is money, time, and space. This is a hardhat and lunch pail kind of world. Gone bad, it is a world of acrimony, suspicion, lawsuits, and rule enforcement.

Language tends to follow need and within the **Ring of roommates** we do a lot of simply moving about. We spend, we schedule, we decorate. We decide to purchase, to alter, to make time for. These functions draw us towards parsimony of language. We use what works.

The **Journey within** feeds on images, feelings, symbols, and connections. Language here is less precise than in roommates and at the same time, far more moving and powerful. A dream in which monsters are encountered cannot be described with the same detachment as you would describe the purchase of a new couch.

In the world of **Deep Friendship** roommate language isn't very interesting. For some it's the only language they have and so intimate conversations become flat lined and boring. This domain doesn't deal with linear pathways and problem solving challenges. The language in the third domain is one you'll borrow from good books, invent as you go, or discover in the heat of exploration. It is a language of wonder, awe, and tenderness.

I have met couples who dealt with the trust issue like private investigators. They are forever examining and re-examining their partner's motives and intentions. They live as if the language of the first domain will suffice in a world entirely different from that one. A little inner work soon will uncover the source of the suspicions. Their work in the journey into intimacy will blossom.

Intimacy requires invitation. Those who create distance through analysis and diagnosis of their partners are not able to relate intimately because neither is invited to be vulnerable within a trusting environment. *All truly intimate conversation is by invitation.* It can never be assumed. Sometimes the invitation is subtle; sometimes it's clear and purposeful.

Most of us agree that intimacy in our relationships is desirable. Few people achieve sustainable intimate relating. In addition to lack of real invitations, there are distractions and seductions that pull us away and fixate our attention on illusions that are far from our hearts.

Some use housework, and some bring homework from the office. Both can be justified, but neither is a legitimate replacement for loving one another. Often they are simply creations that fill time we don't really know what to do with. I am tired of self-righteous explanations for lack of intimacy – my own and others – because they simply are lies or excuses. If you desire to move closer to one another you will. We make time and space for what we truly desire. Excuses are simply a way to keep yourself from facing your fears of being intimate.

What keeps us apart is not housework or office homework. What keeps us apart is *lack of invitation, lack of competency, and non-focused intention.*

B. CREATING SPACE AND TIME

When Bob and Marcy attended their first ***With These Rings*** workshop, **"Intentional Loving,"** they were eager to share their frustration. They each talked about how willing they were but how busy their partner was. "She's cooking dinner, or preparing to cook dinner, or cleaning up, or talking to the kids, or talking to other moms or watching TV," he'd complain. "There's no room for me so I just give up. I go back into my study and play games on the computer."

She feigned patience while he talked. Then, with a half smile on her face, she'd say, "Bob's a baby. Of course I cook and take care of the kids. He's a good provider and it's our agreement that I'll take care of our home. I like doing it. But he's no saint. He'll come up to me and want to talk or make love and it's just not the right time. When I want to talk to him, he's tired or he's on his way out. I can't even talk to him while he's at work. He cuts me off saying 'I can't talk now.'"

They lived in certainty that the "problem" with their intimacy was their partner's. Life in the third domain got sidetracked – like the train tracks that park a train while another passes by – when they had children. But children didn't really do it, either. Lack of competency did.

Our culture's model of marriage teaches that hormonal love will carry us. "Take her out to a nice dinner," or "Buy her a nice piece of jewelry," and everything will be fine. But that isn't so.

C. COMPETENCIES

Competency means that we have to create a model of marriage that works for us. We'll have to go beyond hormones and discover pathways to each other *even when we do not necessarily feel like doing so.*

How might this look for Bob and Marcy? Well, here's one possibility. We did a little role playing and had Bob walk in the front door around 5:30, his normal arrival time at home. We had Marcy cooking, on the phone with another mom, and helping her six-year-old daughter with a panoramic she was building.

Bob: "Hi. How's everybody?"

Marcy: "Excuse me Pam, Bob just got home. Hi, Honey!"

Bob: "What's new?"

Marcy: "Bob I'll be off the phone in a minute. Come here. (She puts Pam on hold and gives him a hug.) Looks him in the eye, "I'm so glad you're home. You look tired. Why don't you grab a shower and get into some comfortable clothes and we can talk over dinner?"

Bob: (nervously) "OK."

This was a simple transition and you might be thinking: "How obvious. So what's new here?" Here's the answer. The competencies we're looking for are not rocket science. This simple *transition* is missed about 90% of the time. Perhaps because it's so obvious it's easy to dismiss.

Competency: *Artful transitioning from one domain to another.*

People in high demand jobs frequently have difficulty recognizing the need for conscious transitions.

Later in the workshop we role played a little more.

(Set up.) The children have been put to bed. We insist on a regular bedtime and our preference is to exchange TV time for reading, projects, or sharing. In this way the children are not hyped up and are more comfortable knowing that they have parents who are primarily interested in their well-being. We believe that a regular bedtime helps the children relax by knowing what the boundaries are.

Our daughter's first grade teacher put it this way:
"All children need boundaries. You get to decide whether someone who loves them teaches them boundaries or someone who doesn't love them has to do it."

This competency sets the stage for the role play because if the parents cannot figure out how to be firm and loving with their children, they are going to have a great deal of difficulty being firm and loving with each other. Or perhaps it's the other way around.

Competency: *Leadership is about taking action with love and firmness.*

So, it's around nine in the evening and Marcy's favorite TV show is about to begin.

Marcy: "We haven't had time to catch up. I'd like to watch this show but I'm willing to tape it so we can talk. How about you?" (Invitation)

Bob: "Well I'm tired now." (Additional information: Bob runs a company and has a long and arduous commute.)

"But I'd like to talk. Let's take a half hour."

Competency: *Begin by agreeing to a limited time, make no promises regarding outcome, and keep to one theme.*

Bob: "I'd like to talk about what's it's like when you call me at work." (Invitation)

Marcy: "You never seem to want me to call you, yet you complain that I don't call enough."

Bob: "At work I'm always complaining about something. There's so much to attend to and it seems I'm always putting out fires."

Role play: active listening. We explain the concept of active listening – carefully feeding back what you hear without editorializing. Ask if you "got" what your partner said.

Bob: "You're saying that I ask you to call, but when you do I don't act like I want you to call. Is that right?"

Marcy: "Yes. Sometimes I just want to connect with you. Sometimes I want to discuss an idea or plans me and the children are making. Sometimes I need your opinion. But you don't make space for me."

Bob: "I see that. It must discourage you from calling me at all."

Competency: *The simple yet profoundly effective art of active listening.*

This simple competency allowed Bob and Marcy to begin to open a pathway to intimate conversation. With a firm schedule for the children and the intentional creation of "space" for the conversation, they started to move beyond blame into actions that would feed their intimacy.

Intimacy is a multi-dimensional subject. Be careful not to think it only includes physical intimacy. The more you see its possibilities, the more likely you are to embrace true intimacy.

My wife said to me: "This is how it works. When you come home tell me how much you missed me, tell me how glad you are you married me, tell me how beautiful I am, and how you appreciate the home I've created with you.... then later, much later, we can talk about roommate issues."

D. COMMITMENT, INTEGRITY, AND TRUST

We make much of faithfulness. Many marriages fail because of one partner's wandering. Often when people talk to me about faithfulness I am reminded of a pet – a faithful dog or a nice kitty. What is faithfulness really all about?

All of us have known betrayal. All of us have been left out, left down, tricked, deceived, manipulated. We know the pain of someone being *not* who we thought they were but someone else entirely. We long for a relationship that we can count on, someone we can completely trust. Someone who would never trick us, lie to us, abandon, or fool us. This longing may be at the heart of much unfaithfulness.

When Judy and Don married she felt incredibly fortunate. She said: "I have found my Moskowitz!" – he was her ideal mate. A man of high standing in the community, a professional, warm and articulate, he was everything she dreamed for in a partner. She knew he was quality, a relational boy scout.

The celebration of their wedding was an event. Friends, family, neighbors all gathered at the beach for what truly seemed a perfect match. Soon Judy was coaching other women on how to find the perfect mate. She considered writing a book about their meeting, their choice of each other, *their* marriage. It was a marriage made in heaven and she would do everything in her power to please Don and to show him how grateful she was to have him.

Don did the same. He regaled friends with stories of 'the perfect match." "We're so compatible," he'd say. "She seems to know what I'm going to say before I say it. The sex is unbelievable. I've never had a relationship like this." He, too, would advise his friends with his newly found knowledge. He'd comment on their choice of women, steer them towards choices that would likely end up with supreme happiness like his own.

I met Judy and Don just after they discovered the affair. They were married just under six years. When they told me how they started out I asked, "What happened?"

Don and Judy's story, though a bit extreme, is not that uncommon. Don told me that her desire to please him began to feel overbearing. He felt boxed in by her idealization of him.

"I'm not that nice a guy, I'm not always there for her, I think I look better than I am."

Judy, on the other hand, tired of praising "a boy in a man's body." "He's so self-centered" she said, "and I can't really please him, ever."

Who had the affair? Well, they both did. They both sought some comfort in someone else and it all took place within a three-week period.

Our desire to match our fantasies will often lead us to project those fantasies onto another person. When they don't meet them we feel cheated.

Faithfulness is about consciousness. It means we are deeply capable of connecting to our own choices and continually validate them. Faithfulness is about being faithful to yourself but not in the old '70s way. It doesn't mean faithful to your whims or impulses. Faithfulness in the end is simply maintaining a coherent connection to the deepest truth of who you are.

Don and Judy's affairs were simply an awkward attempt to pull off their own masks. They didn't divorce. Instead they discovered new resolve to enter the journey into intimacy with integrity, utilizing their considerable passion to clear out the idealizations and ground their relationship at a deeper level.

To fully enter the journey into intimate relating you'll both need to drop your guard. You'll need to explore what commitment is all about. Do not assume that you know and are already committed. The idea of commitment that you have may be very limited.

In intimate exploration, commitment includes the willingness to stay with your partner when they are reluctant, afraid, lost, or sorrowful. Intimate conversations on all levels arouse memories of the past and trigger emotions connected to vulnerability – when perhaps it was not safe to be vulnerable.

Being honest with yourself about your own vulnerabilities, discoveries, confusion, and emotion is critical to this journey as well. Your insistence on your own integrity builds trust even when it's very uncomfortable.

Your partner's integrity will be honored and your commitment will deepen as you trust each other to open in exploration, revelation, and discovery. Knowing that you don't 'know how' to do this is a major contributor to successful intimate conversation.

Before we go any farther, let's look at four kinds of intimacy possible within the journey into intimacy.

E. KNOWING EACH OTHER PSYCHOLOGICALLY

We're not talking textbook here. We're not talking about your attempting to learn the necessary skills to diagnose or analyze each other. In fact, those couples who know and use diagnoses in their relationships are doomed to continually create distance and coldness.

Knowing something of your partner psychologically helps you appreciate the wounds he brings with him, and/or the losses she's suffered in her life. It is to know their "limp" as one of my teachers put it.

If I know that my sweetheart is adopted, I'll know at least something about her abandonment fears. If I know that she has been betrayed by men close to her, I'll know something valuable when she seems cautious or afraid with me. I will not use this information to create a "theory" about her. Rather, I'll use it to frame understanding, to generate empathy, or simply to inquire whether it is relevant within the context of a conflict we're having.

Knowing a man psychologically can include some generalities, like our tendencies toward problem solving when all you want us to do is listen. It can include knowing that we like to withdraw for a time under certain circumstances (into our "caves" as John Gray puts it), and that it usually is not personal.

Psychological knowledge of your partner can include imagining their childhood with them, listening to their stories with a "psychological" ear, and paying attention to their moods.

The more I know of her, the better chance I have to not personalize her changes. Instead I can listen to her words rather than theorizing about her intentions.

Caution: Our same sex friends aren't much help here because they do their own share of generalizing, theorizing, and distancing. If I am going to talk about my marriage with male friends I make sure that they aren't going to run our conversation through their unresolved issues. In other words, I make sure I know a little about them psychologically.

F. EMOTIONAL INTELLIGENCE

There is a nice concept floating around in leadership circles concerning emotional intelligence. It means that tuning in to the emotional components of people – your own and others – makes the difference between a "one way street" type of leadership and a much more highly effective leadership model based on consent, "buy in," and relational integrity.

Here are some questions you might ask yourself:

- What makes my partner's "tail wag?"
- What stirs his passion?
- Exactly what moves her to tears?
- Can I tell the difference between her anger and her frustration?
- Can I see when he's emotionally lost?

- Does our relationship style stress appropriateness or being real?
- Do I embrace passion in myself, and in my partner?

People who have a close working relationship with their feeling responses and have the competence to communicate what they are feeling have knowledge that others who lack that competence do not.

Or, to put it more simply, if you don't know what you're feeling, how am I supposed to relate to you?

Emotional intimacy, like emotionally intelligent leadership, thrives on the development of language to express the feelings that are present. It relies on integrity, perceptiveness, vulnerability, revelation, and the desire to know the other also. This is the foundation of empathy.

If you know grief, you know how difficult words can be. We're in very unfamiliar territory and our instincts to comfort, to say something wise, or to be helpful often seem inadequate. There are things we don't know, can't know, and that are beyond us.

Grief is a state that is loaded with feelings – anger, sorrow, frustration – and exists independently of ordinary social discourse. We can underestimate its power and resilience easily, and somehow think we ought to be able to alleviate its symptoms. But grief is there, has a life of its own, and can intimidate us into anxious attempts at trying to determine its depth. The following is an experience of mine which shows how I learned something about emotional intelligence.

True grief has no voice, no words, no true understanding.
It is the presence of deep loss and its only expression is unrelenting tears.

I was just 30 years old. A Divinity School graduate, lost between my dream of the ministry and a temporary career in a house painting business – a dream I abandoned after serving a church nearly four years. I found that I was relationally incompetent, unable to navigate the complex labyrinth of competing interests, ideas and feelings that every congregation has. So I left and began the painful process of finding myself.

As far as I could tell, the church I served had become a club, stagnant, irrelevant to ordinary people and their extraordinary struggles, and absent in every area of life, save the Sunday morning pews. As far as I could tell. But I was a street kid unfamiliar with the nuances of relationships, quite ignorant of my own emotions, naïve, and young. I was unprepared for the challenges that faced me in the ministry.

I was married and the father of two beautiful girls. We were expecting our third child, a son. The morning the doctor came out to the waiting room with the news that my son had died of cord strangulation approximately an hour before birth broke me in half. The news buckled my knees, vacated my heart, stomach, lungs, vocal cords, and left me gasping on the men's room floor.

Once we were home and carrying the blankets and goodies we'd gathered for the occasion, I had to tell my daughters why Geoffrey was not coming home. We cried together but had no idea what that empty bassinette would mean to us in the months ahead.

Friends stopped by, family called awkwardly offering their words. Slowly I shifted from sorrow to anger. "What are these words?" I thought. What do they know or even care about what we are experiencing? Surely their intentions were good, but their words framed in a lifetime of conservative Christian teaching seemed empty, even somewhat insulting to me.

Here is what they said: "He's in a better place now."

"Better than with me!?" I inwardly screamed.

"God has his reasons" another cooed.

"What possible reason could God have for taking my son from me!? I fumed.

"You're being taught a lesson." One man said. "You disobeyed God when you left the ministry," he explained.

I exploded. "I left the ministry because of folks like you – cold, judgmental and stupid!"

Shaking with rage, frustration, and agonizing sorrow I called a pastor I had met just one time several weeks earlier. I said to him, "You won't remember me but I met you several weeks ago when my family visited your church." He said "I remember you. You're the house painter aren't you?" I told him my son had died.

He said "I'll be right over."

My wife was lying in bed when he came over. He said "How are you?" and then went into the bedroom to sit by her. He said little all day but sat there quietly reading. People came and went. My sad daughters played quietly in their room. My heart was broken. I alternated between feeling like screaming and curling up into a fetal position.

Across the street police cars guarded the home of Sirhan Sirhan, killer of Robert Kennedy. Death, it seemed, was everywhere. Everything I ever learned about faith, every hour spent in studying Scripture, every insight I worked so hard to realize in psychotherapy had escaped me.

Community became a hollow word, vacant and pointless. As the sun sank low in the sky casting our bedroom in a rosy glow, the pastor – tall, lean, Abraham Lincoln in Hush Puppies – looked up from his book. "I better be going," he said.

My wife, always mindful of her role as hostess, said, "I haven't made you anything to eat or drink. All I've done is lie here and cry."

Pastor Lowell Fairley reached over, put his hand on her knee, looked at us both and said, "God is crying too."

Thirty years later those words still feed me.

What he taught me was this: Grief doesn't need a lot of words. Eloquence, advice, cheerleading – all are pointless in the face of profound loss. Presence and a deep integrity are what counts. Emotional and spiritual intimacy are as simple as offering our mere presence, refraining from explaining, and finding genuine interest in the emotional state of the other.

Emotional intelligence can be learned. It will start with your becoming sensitive to the inner country of your inner life. From there you will build relational competency by intelligently tuning in to what you feel and what your partner feels.

I may know about my partner's adoption and understand something of the wound that triggers her fear of abandonment. If I want to be intimately related to her, however I'll also want to tune into her *feelings* about abandonment, whether real or imagined. She may fear abandonment and her fear may open her to a huge vulnerability to her sorrow.

Knowing that, even in the midst of my feeling like she doesn't care about me, will create an intelligent emotional awareness and allow me to *ask* rather than *assume* I know what's going on with her.

By knowing of my losses and grief she'll be able to see my awkwardness in certain social situations differently. She will not jump to conclusions about my attitude but instead will ask and listen. Together we'll intelligently communicate our emotional state and that will change our attitude toward our relationship.

G. SPIRITUAL ATTUNEMENT

Emotional sensitivity and knowledge are closely related to spiritual depth, but they are not the same.

Your spirituality may be the deepest truth that you can communicate to your partner.

Spirituality and intimacy are not often connected. I think that is so because we do not *focus* on the connection. We miss the power and necessity of intimacy – which in its broader aspects is communal – in thinking about spirituality. Marriage is a micro-community and spirit dwells within its agreements, values, and commitments.

Our individual spiritual paths converge in marriage. The values we hold are challenged and shaped by the values our partners hold. Our beliefs do not take shape in isolation from each other, but in dialogue, through challenge and in deep sharing. Marriage offers the opportunity for articulation and maturation of beliefs. There is no room for judgment, superiority, competition, or rejection. We marry our mirrors and they carry much spiritual wisdom for us.

Pay attention to who your partner is, what they "bristle" to, what moves them and what they stand up for.

Many couples who come to us for coaching begin with a story about how little they know one another. This person they married, they say, is not who they thought they were. It shocks some of them when I reply: "Of course they're not. You didn't know who they were when you married them. You had your own images, your projections, your fantasies, wishes, hopes. You largely made your partner up in your head. Hormones will do that. If we really knew who we were partnering with before we started our journey together, we may not have had enough courage to move ahead."

"But, and it's a big *but*, you knew enough. You had a strong hunch about them, something in you resonated to them, you believed that this person was the one."

That is one form of spiritual attunement.

Whether we believe we belong or we don't, whether we are legitimate or are orphans is a spiritual issue as much as a psychological one. What makes us cry, laugh, or rise in fury is as spiritually based as it is emotionally based. What meaning we give to our actions, our lives, our legacies – all are spiritual matters.

We are not islands unto ourselves and our birth and death are as mysterious to us as they are to anyone else. What we do with these mysteries constitutes our spiritual lives.

Knowing your partner spiritually takes courage and inquisitiveness. Most of us haven't had much mentorship here. A great deal of active listening is required. You'll need to suspend your inclinations to critically analyze in order to truly listen. And you'll need to open your hearts to one another.

A man and a woman sit near each other, and they do not long
at this moment to be older, or younger, nor born
in any other nation, or time, or place.
They are content to be where they are, talking or not-
talking.
Their breaths together feed someone whom we do not
know.
The man sees the way his fingers move;
he sees her hands close around a book she hands to him.
They obey a third body that they share in common.
They have made a promise to love that body.
Age may come, parting may come, death will come.
A man and a woman sit near each other;
as they breathe they feed someone we do not know,
someone we know of, whom we have never seen.

- Robert Bly

H. PHYSICAL PRESENCE

Unfortunately for many of us, our culture has so dumbed down physical intimacy that it is almost like reading the Bible after being in church for forty years. We have trouble hearing the words as if for the first time.

Presumption is the killer of intimacy. A man I know told his wife of 18 years this: "I do not know how to make love to you. I've known for 30 or 40 years "how" to make love but tonight I realize I don't have a clue." They embraced in tears, but the tears were tears of relief. She confessed that she didn't know how, either. That night they began a new chapter in their journey into intimacy.

We touch out of habit or desperation, but rarely out of pure tenderness instinctually giving the substance of love we have known for so long but perhaps forgotten. I have known hugs where hands felt like claws and I have known hugs so natural I knew there was genuine loving in them. Physical presence brings with it the emotional tonality of the moment. It brings a sense of your psychology and your spiritual resonance.

What we don't know may be the most important ingredient in finding a pathway to renewed physical intimacy. Being aware that we don't know humility and vulnerability yet daring to ask, our tenderness and care beginning the conversation. Focus on your loving rather than whether you're getting what you need.

Physical intimacy is not goal oriented, but many of us act as if it is. You can discover great joy in exploration and discovery. Putting assumptions aside allows you to find out who your partner is. Allow room for non-goal oriented touching, talking, questioning, and sharing.

Someone told me recently that taking care of her body was the most important gift she could bring to her partner. She meant watching the foods she eats because they determine energy or lack of it, regular exercise, attention to the clothes she wears around the house, and care of her skin. This woman doesn't use alcohol or tobacco, is careful about skin care, eats foods that work well with her physical needs, and stretches several times daily. She's a lovely woman and her physical presence is indeed compelling.

She and her partner like to give foot and hand massages, back and shoulder massages, and facials to each other. They do this not with a goal in mind, but simply because they like touching each other.

"How do you get your partner to touch if they aren't used to it?" This question was from a mid-thirties man who had been married a short time (maybe 3 or 4 years) and told me on a break that his partner had been molested as a young girl and been "phobic" about touching ever since.

Of all our defenses, our physical ones are probably the hardest to change since they mostly have slipped into being habits and we've learned to call them by other names. "I just don't feel like being close tonight," or "It's the way you approach me," or "I'm tired," or "I'm not a night person." Each of these may be valid, but quite often are a cover for a learned response that protects the individual from exposure or vulnerability.

We begin by slowing the process way down. We ask couples to refrain from making love for a week, a month, or whatever period of time seems manageable. Then we have them explore, ask questions. We might have them practice active listening, have them talk about their love for each other – all within a firm agreement that there will be no physical lovemaking.

Creating space for the defenses to relax slowly is a first step. Acknowledging past pain, fear, isolation, and vulnerability is next. Honoring your partner's presence, knowing something about them emotionally, spiritually, psychologically and physically sets the stage for moving from distance to intimate conversation.

This third journey is a wonderland, a garden, a never-ending source of delight. Do not be afraid to bring candles, poetry, silk, and fine music to any of the conversations where your intent is to know each other more intimately than you did yesterday.

We've created several CDs to help you here. They are called *The Marriage Conversation* and offer short stories with a point followed by questions to help you get conversation going. They are available on our website.

Getting a sense of what the three journeys offer will help you understand competition between the two of you, and why it is so deadly. In good marriages we rarely find better or worse; we more often find differences. Notice, too, that one domain doesn't trump another (they are not hierarchal). They are complementary to each other.

We know we've only dipped our toes and yours in the deep, deep waters of intimate relating. There's much more. Your interest and competence will grow as you intelligently open to your own and your partner's inner work.

Don't be afraid to involve a wisdom partner – a spiritual counselor, therapist, or wise friend – to hold you accountable and to keep the work focused.

I. CREATING SHARED VISION FOR INTIMACY

Life together as roommates is shaped and vitalized by the quality of each partner's inner life, or what may be called their inner journey connection. Looking back at Theseus for a moment, the work of running the kingdom, clearly in the 'outer journey' domain, was off-limits for discussion. The queen ruled and she was not open to Theseus' input. She lived in domain one, dominated it, and saw no reason to include her husband in any significant way. Many marriages are like this. One partner makes all the decisions and the other complies. They go on, never facing the imbalance and the resulting lack of intimacy.

But Theseus was growing in his awareness of himself as a young man and began to see that he could no longer be a "man by night and a boy by day" I like that phrase because it captures the dilemma of power in one domain and irrelevance in another.

Some women feel like they are asked to be a "woman at night" yet defer every major discussion to their man by day. They haven't seen a path by which they can self actualize or realize their individuality and be a fully functional partner.

I've known men who complain of being "a well-dressed paycheck." They feel patted on the head and far down the chain of command when it comes to family decisions.

A complaint is a call to consciousness for both partners. Negotiating differences in decision making depends upon competence in embracing conflict. If the couple begins to develop the competency to embrace conflict, they can open up a conversation that invites individual gift and genius into their strong desire to partner.

Theseus, aware of his intention, leaves the kingdom run by women and continues on the way to meet his father.

He is continuing his separation from his mother. It's not as simple as it sounds, and is a more common challenge than we admit. Many men in our time are "mother based," meaning they have little viable or working relationship with their own masculinity. They live as servants to a mode of being that denies their legitimacy as men. The women they marry suffer and often refer to these husbands as "one of the children," disguising their contempt as a joke.

Women whose mothers lost their voice before they were born may forever wander aimlessly – their own meaning, gifts, or worth eluding them.

When they partner they may do very well externally (domain one). They may be very successful financially or professionally. Their capacity to enter domain two and begin the inner journey may be limited by their fear of the depth of their wounds.

Creating a shared vision with your partner will be challenging if you lack the depth of experience to articulate one. Struggling to create a shared vision in the first domain where money may equal power, space may mean safety, and time may translate into significance can stall at the intersection of our wounds and our desires.

Shared vision is not about compliance or conformity, and is not about a rigid set of goals. It is a shared valuing of ideals in which a couple successfully makes conscious their individual aspirations in the realm of the "kingdom" they are establishing.

Within the journey into intimacy, shared vision reflects a conscious appreciation and shared valuing of intimate relating. It may mean that both partners sense the importance of conscious effort, the centrality of embracing conflict, and the tender vulnerability of exposure that this journey offers.

We sense that our partner's inner work is sacred, and he/she acknowledges the same for us. In doing so we will leave lots of space for personal exploration and will honor it by not intruding or questioning their integrity.

PART IX

INTIMACY EVOLVING: THREE POSSIBLE MARRIAGES WITHIN MARRIAGE

A. HIERARCHIES

Some people think they are more relationally "pure" than their partners. I've heard couples argue like this: "All she cares about is how much money I make or what's in the bank." "Sure he makes a good living, but he's cold." "If I had wanted a domestic I would have married one." "He's obsessive about his projects but he spends virtually no time with us."

These are attempts to establish hierarchies. The person complaining believes, for example, that their agendas trump their partner's agenda. They elevate their point of view to a form of self-righteous proclamation. "Things would be much better around here if you only saw the world the way I do." Or as psychologist and author Bruce Derman says, "We'd have a good relationship if it wasn't for you."

Journeys do not work that way. Every intimate experience you have can be found in the way you work together, plan together, play together, or handle money together. The first domain is a hardhat and lunch pail kind of place but that doesn't mean it's a soul-less place.

The second domain is all about inner life, but it doesn't take place in a kind of mythic realm that is disembodied and apart from the relationship you're working in. The inner work we do transforms the quality of our shared lives in the outer world just as our competencies in money, space, and time communicate our values and our desires.

Several years ago a father who was successful financially and well known in his profession asked me for a consultation regarding his sixteen-year-old son. He was in trouble in school, somewhat violent (although in this family getting angry was considered "violent"), and the father believed he had started hanging out with the "wrong crowd" in school.

In our first meeting, the father told me that his son (having just parked the new Porsche the father had given him for his sixteenth birthday under the second story plate glass window of the family "rec" room) "stormed in while I was on the phone with a client and demanded we talk." 'I need to talk to you now!' he said. I said, 'Wait a minute. I'll be through in a minute.'

"He wouldn't wait. Furious, he picked up the new television set we just bought for the rec room and hurled it through the plate glass window. It landed on his Porsche parked below and caused considerable damage. I didn't know whether to call the police or smack him."

As the father talked, his son, an athletic looking 6'2" or so, looked at the floor. His neck, and then his cheeks were reddening. He shook his foot.

I said to him, "What happened?"

He said, "He told you. Why do I have to repeat it? He's right. It happened like he said."

I asked him, "Did he leave anything out?"

"Yea," he said. "He left me out. He always leaves me out. He thinks his &*!#@*&!!... presents are all there is to being a father. He's either at work or on the phone. He expects nothing but progress reports from me. He's the same way with my mother."

This cryptic eloquence just burst out like it had been cooking inside him for years, suffering these thoughts until he could no longer contain them. When the dam broke, he let go of his frustration and loneliness.

If you were evaluating this from a domain one perspective, you could easily reach the conclusion that this son needed consequences for his "off the end of the ruler" (another father favorite) behavior. Clearly there was nothing that justified such a violent reaction.

Some might suggest medicating the boy. Another might recommend calling the police. Seen from the perspective of a courtroom, the son might be guilty and deserve a sentence.

A great deal of our cultural perspective on young men looks like this. We ask that they be socialized to fit in with our expectations. We want them to be "nice," "appropriate," or "compliant."

We miss the deep truth young men carry in their passion. Have you ever wondered why some have to have speakers installed in their cars that simply drown out the noise of the world? (Later on I'll offer an image related to a garden that offers one way to imagine what goes on with youth.)

This young man knew something and he wasn't going to let it go. I started asking the father some questions. What did he know about his son's life? Did he know who his son's best friends were? Had he spent any time with them? I asked if he knew what time his son came home from school. "About 3:30 or 4, depending on whether he's with his druggy friends," the father replied.

The son started to react, but then said, "Oh, the hell with it. He'll never get what you're saying." So far, I pointed out, I hadn't said much. I was just asking questions. "Right," the son replied, "but I know where you're going. You're going to convince my father that he's clueless about me. He is. But he won't listen to you. He doesn't listen to anybody."

I asked the father if he ever called the son when he got home from school. "Look," he said, "this is about him, not about me. If you want to make me look like a bad father, go ahead. But that is not what we came here for. We came here to help him out. I know how therapists think. It's all the parents' fault. But this is not a deprived kid. In fact, I've given him everything a kid could want. He's ungrateful and his druggy friends are putting ideas into his head. And if you think you are going to help him by giving him sympathy, you're wrong. We won't be back. I came here to get some good advice. Apparently all I'm going to get is 'it's all your fault.'"

With that he started out of the office. The son stayed. Soon we heard the father's sports car roar off. The son was silent for a while. Then, slowly getting up, he looked at me with huge tears rolling down his face. "How do you deal with that?" he said and left.

If you computed the value of the father's gifts against the cost of his time you might come up with something like this: Let's say the sports car and new television set cost $60,000. Perhaps that would equal, at his billing rate, thirty or forty days of his professional time.

Let's speculate: instead of the gifts, he offered his son his time. "We can take a week every two months for the next year or so" he might say. That would be a value that the son could experience directly and it might help him to get his own values in order.

In order to do this the father would have to be willing to do some domain two (inner) work. He'd look at how it came to be that his career and fortune came to be of greater value than spending time with his son. He'd look at his fears – perhaps of being insignificant, of failure, or of not providing adequately for his family.

He'd have to develop a partnership with his wife in which they learned how to be open, genuine, and empathic with each other. He'd have to learn how to embrace conflict so that, instead of conflict leading to being walled off from one another, it would lead to deeper understanding.

This is a tall order for a warrior/ man who succeeds in the world on the strength of his wit, aggressiveness, and determination.

Going from the outer world to the world of relationships requires familiarity with the three journeys, considerable competency in transitions, knowledge in the needs of others, and awareness of love.

If he could recognize the longing in his son, this father might recognize the emptiness in himself. Life in the first domain can be seductive because the rewards are tangible and immediate. Toys are great. The metrics of this world assure us that what we're doing is meaningful.

This is not so in our inner worlds. The first domain is pretty much one dimensional. The inner world is a maze. To go "down and in," as some describe the inner journey, is to lose your outer world bearings. You may lose them for a short or a long time, but the world of images, values, history, and emotion is a mythic world. The rules that govern travel there are not the rules of this world.

We could imagine several different conversations between this father and this son if they could grasp the fact that neither was ready to fully listen to the other. There was a kind of enchantment – neither was truly open and both had settled on a theory of what the other was capable of.

Had the son engaged the father in his awareness of their relationship prior to the buying of the sports car, there may have been an entirely different kind of conflict. He may have introduced his need for more time. He could have expressed appreciation for his father's generosity but declined the car and instead asked for a less expensive one to trade the value for time with his father. He could even invite his mother and father into a conversation about values in this family. He could have, but he didn't.

We are all only as conscious as we *can* be. I use the idea of journeys to capture a sense of intention, growing awareness, discovery, obstacles and promise.

Neither the father nor the son was "bad" or "good." The son isn't a victim of the father and the father is not an unappreciated good guy. They were missing each other in a major way and the explosion, drama, and angst were huge calls for attention to the vulnerability of their relationship.

Couples often get lost in the same way the father and son did. Home improvements can do it or a major purchase can trigger it as well. The journey in the outer world – the first domain – uses money, space and time to shape the quality of our lives and our major means of communication.

The inner journey is not more important than the outer journey. Many people are skillful and conscious in their dealing with money and consciousness. Some clearly can see how money communicates, know its symbolic importance, and are tuned in to its shape shifting value. They seem to integrate an inner relationship with money with an awareness of love and value.

Nor is the outer journey just about the "things in our lives," as one woman at a workshop expressed it. The journey looks like a cooperative effort in which we establish our "kingdom." We use the materiality of life – money, space, even time – to shape and express what we often cannot articulate in our inner world. Consciousness and a shared vision for our lives together as "roommates plus" is the result of successfully combining these two worlds.

We can see that the journeys intersect and influence one another. It's clear that work in one will affect work in another and it is also clear that competition is useless. Your strength can and should complement the weakness in your partner. The way we feed each other is by honoring and listening to the work and insight our partner brings to relationship.

It might be time now to lay a sequence out and take a little peek behind the curtain of ***With These Rings***: *The Marriage Conversation* model. We'll look at how domains need rings, and rings prepare us for journeys.

B. DOMAINS, RINGS, AND JOURNEYS

When couples seek help to enliven their marriages or to address chronic relational pain, they are looking for skills and tools that would be useful in transforming what they know into relational experiences they hoped for. They have an idea of what's possible or they wouldn't seek help in the first place.

Transformation of old patterns, deep wounds, chronic habits into new life takes a belief that it is possible to change plus some images that promote change. Getting to your feelings helps but isn't sufficient for long lasting transformation.

We introduced the ideas of domains, rings and journeys as a possible model for you so that you could see for example the difference between the wedding and setting up house, and a marriage where a vision for this life is shared and consciously worked towards.

We see a progression in relationship from living in domain awareness – our house, our things, our jobs – to the ring of deep commitment to each other's well being as well as the establishment of our micro community in the midst of the larger community. It takes vision to do this.

The progression from domain to ring to journey further extends awareness of the possibilities offered this couple and additionally carries the idea of the true adventure of a relationship shared over a lifetime.

Here are some images to help you imagine this progression:

If you're in a conversation about re-decorating the living room, buying a new car or brainstorming your schedules so that all that you do gets handled, you're in the first domain.

If the same conversation emphasizes the *agreements* you live by, relates back to your *commitments* to share the work of parenting, or acts as financial partners in decisions regarding large expenses, then you're in the first *ring* of the marriage conversation.

We function practically – making decisions, scheduling, budgeting – and we do this in a logical, sequential, and hopefully, reasonable way. Our intentions to value each other's point of view, to consider each other's feelings, to agree to work things through when we can't agree, to honor each other's wisdom – all relate to our commitment to love one another. We call that commitment a ring because it sets apart our *intention* from our *behavior*. But beyond the domain of practical living and the ring of mutually agreed participation or involvement with each other is the notion that together we're also *going somewhere.*

If you are *sharing* with each other and *exploring* the impact of your personal histories on spending patterns or use of time, your parents' sensitivity or insensitivity about use of space, the feelings you experience when the two of you talk about money, or time or space, or your dreams of establishing your kingdom, you're in the first *journey* of marriage. This journey is lifelong and will offer many challenges along the way.

These three concepts underlie the possibility of transforming your marriage and play an important role in developing a strategy of intimate relating.

Domains, rings, and journeys clarify communication and they help to clarify conflict by locating your point of reference.

---

1. *Roommates*

When we're in the first *domain* – scheduling time for example – we might prefix this brainstorming conversation with a "heads up": "Look, we're just talking about this, right?" We use this as a kind of flag – we're talking, but not trying to come to an agreement. We're exploring all options, even silly ones. This contextualizes what we're doing and invites both of us to leave our agendas and possible defensiveness (our personal private detective) outside the door.

The agreement also reduces competitiveness, the triggering of who's working harder or sacrificing more.

If you're in the first *ring* you might be examining the assumptions, promises, and commitments you bring to this conversation. I know a couple who had chronic and heated arguments about their children's activities and the challenge of getting them to each event and back on time. I drew on a white board as the intensity increased demonstrating the first ring in marriage. Quite suddenly, she got it.

"I work under the assumption of shared parenting," she said. "We talked a lot about that before we married. I just realized – I knew this, but it just really hit me – that that agreement was based on both of us working and sharing the financial responsibilities of our lives. Since we have had our children, I have reduced my work load by about 80% while Scott has increased his substantially. Even so, I was still relating to Scott as if we were under the old agreement."

Catching an image of their agreement, the first ring, allowed her to re-frame their dialogue around schedules. It was an old agreement and it no longer applied to the life they were living. But some of it did. They both believed in shared parenting and they both worked hard – perhaps too hard – in establishing their financial viability.

Realizing the change of circumstance opened the possibility for visioning a life (and therefore an agreement) that would more accurately reflect their current situation. This shared journey represents truthful deliberation and consent around shared intentions.

But how do we bring the fullness of who we are, where we've been, and who we're becoming into the conversation? I'm reminded here of icebergs. They only show a small portion of their mass. Like that tip of the iceberg, our daily personality reveals only a snapshot of who we are.

2. *Inner work*

The *inner domain* notices that we have dreams, aspirations, and fantasies. It notices, too, that our personal histories carry meaning that is not always evident, that there is more to loving than hormones, that we change over time, that poetry, music and art contain deep symbolism for us and that gender awareness is a legitimate topic for exploration. This domain is virtually endless in offering opportunities for exploration.

The *ring* of inner work defines our commitment *to* and our capacity *for* inner work. Some people are very hungry for inner knowledge, some are not so interested, but all *have* an inner life. Some couples who seek coaching have very limited goals for their marriage. They may want to create a money management style that works, or they may want coaching on how they approach conflict.

We observe that each couple has different needs and aspirations regarding their pursuit of consciousness. We're not making value judgments. What we want to emphasize is a distinction: domains describe the territory; and rings describe the value placed on commitment, agreement, and intention.

The *journey* of inner work carries the idea of movement, of uncovering, descent, exploring and revealing. It is a journey in every sense of the word with the exhaustion that comes from toiling too long, the exhilaration we know upon seeing a new vista, also defeat, frustration, the most tender of discoveries, missed turns, and the poignancy of knowing something you did not know yesterday.

Journeys give shape to the visions we carry, share the meaning of the adventure, and open us to possible discovery beyond our perception.

The substance of our work in these first two domains provides a foundation for the joys of life in the journey of relating intimately with one another.

3. *Intimacy*

The *third domain* describes the arena of conscious intimate sharing. This domain includes four dimensions of intimacy: psychological, spiritual, emotional, and physical intimacy.

The third *ring* holds us to our word, the word spoken in the beginning. It is the words of love with which we (innocently I think) gave ourselves to one another. The idea of "with this ring I thee wed" carries a deep sense of intimate commitment. And this ring, symbolized by the ring you wear, reminds us of purpose and intention.

The first principle in our philosophy of marriage is this:
I have a deep need to love and I choose to love you.

The third *journey* evokes the quality of sharing deeper levels of intimate relating. Both of you opening to areas of exploration that may not be entirely comfortable or even safe. What you always thought you'd keep to yourself can be revealed on this third journey. Here you can reclaim a loving that only yesterday was vital and alive.

This journey is characterized by *invitation.* It is never assumed. The primary need is deep respect for one another. While the first journey is described largely by necessity, the second by inner need, the third is characterized by wonder. Together they describe the substance of marriage and help us to understand that while weddings mark a beginning, there is within each journey another marriage waiting to be realized.

4. *Old paradigms and new creations*

The invitation to take marriage seriously is not yet an irresistible one. Our old paradigm of marriage runs towards complacency. Some of us fret about it, but then blame our mediocrity on the wrong things. "People don't commit anymore," or, "It's the values of this generation," or "they've just made it too easy to divorce." Even if these things were true, they still wouldn't account for the large number of marriage failures. I'll say it again: *People don't marry thinking that they'll divorce* and most divorces aren't about frivolousness Divorce happens for a lot of reasons, but one major reason is that the paradigm we live with simply no longer compels our loyalty and attention.

If the feelings recess we may think the marriage is over. If the joy of the wedding has long passed we ask, "Is this all there is?" When we chronically argue over money, sex, or children we may think, "I must have made a mistake marrying this person."

Our current paradigm contributes to a 'dummying down' of the conversation relying as it does on romance, medieval agreements and wedding parties. We can each create a new way to take on each of the above scenarios but *we need a vision of what marriage can be,* rather than our fear of what it isn't. Take a look down the road of your own journey into intimacy and ask, "What does this marriage want to look like in a year, in five years, in twenty?"

Ask yourselves, "How does our vision for shared intimacy relate to our individual visions for inner work?" And "does our vision for life together as roommates feed or starve our vision for shared intimacy?"

Beyond seeing the possibilities of embracing conflict and of having a well-defined philosophy of marriage, beyond reconnecting to your own garden of Eden, beyond even the exhilaration of communicating within consciousness of the three journeys – beyond all this – lies another promise.

Each journey has within it the possibility of a deeper connection than we thought possible. Each journey contains a marriage that can unite and connect us, challenge us, and inspire us to a deeper realization of intimacy than we've ever dreamed possible.

5. The marriages within each journey

To reclaim your love is to do more than create a loving relationship that will feed and nourish you and your partner as well as your family. Hidden within each journey is a promise for new levels of intimacy, the possibility for deeper bonding, and the realization of love manifested in a way you've never known.

When we counsel couples who appear bitter, discouraged, negative, or depressed, we think it is because the promises that they knew with all the possibilities of partnering, were never realized. You might say they are realizing, in their depression, what they've missed.

We believe that each of us has the opportunity to change that at this very moment in our lives.

Not only that but somewhere buried deep within your initial intention was a promise to together work to realize the promise you signed up for when you said "I do."

There has never been a time when more resources have been available. Coaches, counselors, therapists, books, tapes, and articles abound. There are workshops, seminars, internet-based resources, church programs, and library programs. Some states even offer government programs aimed at helping couples find a better path in their marriages.

It's really not so hard to get started. All you have to do is agree that the work of discovery, with its uncertainty and even its fear, is preferable to an auto-pilot relationship where nothing ever changes. You also will have to jointly agree to commit to stay with it.

A path to a deeper realization of intimacy *in each domain* offers a sense of another level of partnering. The ***With These Rings*** paradigm offers a major addition to our notions of partnering.

Once you "get" the idea of the three journeys, you can use it to clarify communication, reframe conflict, open new pathways to intimacy, re-ground your love and create a philosophy of marriage that will sustain and support your work together and your love.

C. THE FIRST JOURNEY BECOMES A MARRIAGE

Although most of us imagine that life as roommates is a linear, practical, logical participation in the daily business of life, it is that but also more than that.

Think of the way we compartmentalize things. We had "my" children and "her" children. "My" money, "her" money. "My" house, "her" house.

Before we married we were neatly separate and the idea of marriage challenged us. How would we do it? What would it look like to buy a house together, sort out our finances, be fair to one another, have our individual parenting styles, yet share fully in the responsibilities?

We spent several hours with an accountant who was enormously helpful about the numbers but clueless about the challenges we presented. We decided to marry even though the path was far from clear.

Over the first months and even the first two or so years of our marriage, my wife and I avoided the kind of conversation that we invite couples into immediately. But as our children grew, we were increasingly forced to deal with creating a shared vision that would accurately reflect who we were and how we loved.

One day as we stumbled into a heated argument about how much we'd spend on Christmas, I saw her differently than I had before. In that moment she ceased being my adversary – the one who would spend us into bankruptcy – and instead I saw her deep generosity and desire to create abundance with all our children. She wasn't foolish. She was expansive and my history had trouble allowing for that.

That recognition was another beginning, a marriage in this first domain now looked possible. I'd call it the beginning of empathy. Not the usual kind – for the way she felt, etc. – but empathy and recognition for who she was and honor for her attitudes about money.

Within the first journey we go from simply dealing with money to pay bills and buy things to slowly awakening to the reality that money means something different to each of us. The way we talk about money, our images of success and failure, providing and supporting, our ideas about leisure, home, freedom and security represent very different realities to each of us.

Empathy is a quality which takes some time to truly manifest in a relationship. Empathy around domain one issues moves a couple from roommates to partners. In that movement, a deeper bonding is possible. There is a marriage within that domain waiting to happen.

Francine and Jack competed about nearly everything, but their biggest "thorn" was how each spent money. Jack criticized Francine for spending extravagantly on the children's clothes while she thought his occasional night out was unnecessary and indulgent. Often their bills were late in being paid, they were in agony over unplanned expenses, and they weren't saving any money.

They were in an early stage of journey awareness. When a therapist friend suggested to them that the initial stage of marriage was about to end and a new phase was waiting to begin, they wanted to know more.

Soon the therapist had them talking about their images and needs. Francine's childhood losses and her keen sense of wanting a better life for her children became a conversation about her love for Jack and the children they shared. The conversation developed into an empathic brainstorming about how they could parent effectively and generously and at the same time look to the future they were building. Jack could buy into her desire to give them an abundant childhood if he could believe she related to their money as a finite resource.

When Jack explained what a night out with friends really meant to him, a deep need to stay connected to good friends and not disappear into his marriage like his older brothers had done, Francine began to understand his vulnerability and his strength. His love for her was evident, and his determination to live his life fully made sense.

Their lives in domain one began to look like shared vision around money and future. They were at the beginning of a "new 'marriage" in this domain, one that would both feed their souls and ground their daily lives.

This "marriage" would do well with an upgrading of their vows, the creation of a shared vision statement (in domain one) and the possible creation of a holy moment by memorializing it with a simple ceremony.

When we are truly present with one another, all opinions, theories, hypotheses, diagnoses, analyses, criticisms, and other things that cause distances are absent from our relationship.

D. THE INNER JOURNEY OFFERS A SURPRISE

Rumi, the twelfth century poet, noticed that we look for lovers everywhere but the truth is that our lovers are not out there, they are "in each other all along." He meant that the soul mate we seek is waiting within us. They are a shadow, a presence we can feel, but never see. Some use the word "inner twin" to identify this lover. Poets have spoken of her or him for a long time but in our time we've given that sweet presence almost entirely to a fantasy of the 'outer lover.'

Since at birth we begin our journey into consciousness without knowing whether we're male or female, some think that life is a process in which we discover who we are as reconnect with that silent lover we split off from long ago.

Our culture helps us split off the not-so-conscious aspects of our twin – our masculine side or our feminine presence - by focusing us on the outer world. *Reconnecting will change the way you relate to your real world partner.*

You'll begin to withdraw your projections. You'll find yourself identifying more easily with your partner's struggles. You'll ease into competencies you didn't realize you had. You'll be emotionally and psychologically more flexible and your emotional range will expand.

If I can connect to my inner soul mate I will lose a great deal of desperation. I'll be able to relate to a woman like a grown-up man who has a heart, is competent in loving, is stable in commitment and who feels loved just the way he is. I will not come to her asking her to save me, rescue me, make me worthy or feel loved. I will not come to her as a project.

This discovery looks like an inner marriage because it is, in a real sense, a marriage of inner and outer self. This "marriage" is so important psychologists that have named it. It's called *Hieros Gamos.* Your dreams will confirm it and guide you there.

E. THE INTIMATE JOURNEY INTO DEEP BONDING

In the movie *On Golden Pond*, Henry Fonda's character goes hunting for strawberries and gets lost in the woods. As time passes his wife, played by Katharine Hepburn, becomes worried. Finally he stumbles into the kitchen somewhat disheveled and looking frightened. He says "I was afraid I couldn't find my way back to you."

I'll go out on a bit of a limb here. Women are "home" to a man; as men may appear as "the world" to a woman. Within the journey into deeper levels of intimacy there is not only the possibility of leaving behind a good deal of wasted time arguing but also a continual sharpening of appreciation for what your partner really means to you.

Marriages do not need to become boring and people don't need to fall out of love. We have discovered that love keeps calling us to discover *who we are to each other* even as we discover new dimensions of *who we are*. We just have to be willing explorers.

The marriage hidden within this journey is a soul-to-soul marriage that has faced the realities of each partner's gifts, emotional range, intellectual talent, spiritual depth, and physical tonality. You have also found a way to include the recognition of your limits, the limits of this life (we are mortals), as well as the gifts contained within those limits.

This love goes far beyond what we were able to see at the wedding. This lovemaking is kaleidoscopic and far from the one-dimensional lovemaking or our youth. This marriage is a deeply felt, spiritual reflection of souls in communication.

I am grateful to a friend who, upon reading the above two paragraphs asked for more. She said this: "Are you saying that 'marriage' within the third journey is important because it calls us to open to a fuller realization of what both of our loving can offer each other? We, my husband and I, are just beginning to realize that we stopped imagining what love offers a long time ago. Now we're excited for the future. I can't wait to move into all three marriages."

PART X

MANIFESTING CONSCIOUS LOVING

A. LOVING OUT LOUD

The philosopher and novelist Emile Zola said this: "If you asked me what I came into the world to do I will tell you. I came to live out loud."

What is the point of being married if it isn't finding a path to love someone with all that you are, to actually make a difference, to create a micro-community that nourishes you and your family, and to positively impact the community you are in?

Loving out loud is at the center of it all because our spiritual, psychological, emotional, and physical well-being dry up if we can't find a pathway to love. Marriage isn't the only form in which this can take place of course, but it is the focus of our work for now.

Manifesting your love requires the faith that you do love and the confidence that you are lovable. Loving someone is not the walk in the park it was when hormones, newness, and fascination reigned. Loving requires continual reconnection to the heart of that kind of love as well as focused intention. It requires taking on your own ego, dealing with your own blind spots, grieving your wounds, taking care of past business – all the efforts of self healing that you can embrace.

It also requires forgiveness. Here's a little story:

He was on his way to speak to an audience of about 150 business men and women. A busy professional speaker, he became increasingly anxious as he approached the location, so much so that he pulled into a McDonald's parking lot to reflect and to gain some perspective.

"I'm just not good enough for these people," he thought. "I don't know enough, I'm not an expert in their business challenges, and I certainly haven't prepared as well as I could." He sat there for a moment and then, unexpectedly, tears ran down his cheeks. He was thinking: "I want to give them my best. I want their time with me to be worthwhile. I don't know that I have enough to give all that they certainly deserve."

He stayed with those feelings. Then he started to forgive himself. Soon he was thinking "Forgive me for not being all that I possibly could be for you." The cloud lifted. He started his car and went to the meeting.

After being introduced, he stood and looked out at the faces of those seated in the room. There was kindness, expectation, some laughter, certainly acceptance. He said to them: "Forgive me. I wanted to bring you wonderful business insights, but I only brought what I know. I wanted to inspire you, but I am only going to give you what I have in my heart. You certainly deserve the most informed speaker, the ablest coach, the most eloquent presenter. I brought me. Forgive me." He said all this without affectation. He wasn't seeking their approval, but was reminding himself out loud that who he was and what he brought had to be good enough.

In partnership the challenge is similar. We need to connect the dots and accept who I am and what I bring as "good enough." This is not a call for passive self-indulgence but instead relates to those of you who are forever questioning your love or doubting the way you come towards your partner.

I am talking of deep self-acceptance.

Manifest means moving out of the shadows and the safety your love has lived in and allowing your loving to 'walk around in your house.' It means leaving the safety of caution, sophistication, analysis of others, and the protection of your ego and exposing to yourself and to those you love the depth, texture, and colors of your loving.

B. ACCOUNTABILITY

To love out loud will mean you are no longer hiding. You will have to become accountable for the way your love shows up instead of custom designing your loving to fit the occasion. "I'm not passive," a man I know joked, "I just don't want to be held accountable for my thoughts or actions."

Loving out loud removes your mask. Can you guess why you began hiding behind a mask of "appropriateness" in the first place? Can you remember being shamed for being too loving, too real, or too anything else? Our mask building starts early. School is a good teacher of mask building. So is church. But they'd both have a lot more trouble succeeding if our own families didn't stress appropriate behavior so strongly.

Much childlike enthusiasm is misunderstood, misperceived, or even misdiagnosed. Some parents have their doctors prescribe medicine for their children when someone at school says they are hyperactive. Perhaps it's the school classroom – a hypoactive environment – that creates an environment where healthy children appear to be too active. The deficit in attention that the ADD diagnosis refers to may really be an adult deficiency in attending to the full spectrum of a child's needs. But, that's another book.

Learning to mute your loving happens in many different settings. What's important here is to know the stakes of loving out loud. If you decide you want a marriage that sings, you'll have to learn to be fully accountable for all the wacky, tender, inappropriate, amazing, wonderful ways that your love naturally occurs in relationship to the one you love.

It might be helpful to look at love's manifestation through the lenses of the three journeys.

If we started with how your love is manifest in the outer world of money, space, and time, we'd begin, I think, with what may sound like a dry and academic concept. But it is actually full of juice for opening and vitalizing relationships. Take a look at how you "talk" to each other through the medium of money. Are you conscious of your love when making financial decisions? Are your gifts for each other "duty dates" with the calendar or do they come from a careful integration of value and loving attention?

Most of what we do *not* see of love is hidden behind the strategies of avoidance, denial, projection, and the inability to live in the present. If you can escape accountability to yourself, if you can let yourself drift into "maybe

I just don't love her/ him" or "I think I've fallen out of love," etc., then you're lost and you will not be able to manifest your love.

In his book *The Power of Now*, Eckart Tolle calls this your "pain body." You've decided to let your past wounds and betrayals become a firewall against living your love.

You could start with a truth session (perhaps invite a therapist) in which you honestly answer the questions – who did you choose to love, who do you love. When asking these questions I'm not suggesting that you are searching for the *feeling* of love but simply to hold yourself accountable to yourself about your own choices.

If you can answer those two questions about your love you can go to the next step. If you admit to yourself (sounds strange doesn't it?) that your partner is the one you've chosen to love and that you, in fact, do love her although at this moment the feeling is not present, then ask another simple question. What stands in the way of my love flowing towards her?

Use caution here. You'll be tempted, as we all are, to offer yourself a diagnosis and/or analysis of her/him. "If only he was more…" "If only she didn't …" Stop that! Replace that with a repeat of the question, "What stands in *my* way of my love flowing?

Accountability starts with yourself. It quickly involves your partner, however, because admitting your love for her is only one step away from admitting and claiming your love *to* her. This is an important starting point in healing distance.

This conversation can ground you with both of you admitting and claiming your love for each other. The next step is the creation of a vision for your life together.

Love seeks no cause beyond itself and no fruit; it is its own fruit, its own enjoyment. I love because I love; I love in order that I may love.

St. Bernard

C. STAYING CURRENT IN THE FIRST JOURNEY: SHARED VISION

You may think you've already done this but we have found a great need for upgrades in relationships. Shared Vision 1.0 will look a lot different than the 3.0 version. In the domain of roommates, everything keeps changing. We buy a house; we outgrow the house. Our cars wear down, there's sickness, changes of employment, new babies, and all kinds of unexpected bonuses and challenges.

Love evolving will look like a continuous sense of discovery. You find strengths, talents, even genius in each other you didn't even know were there. You are individuating, learning, evolving, manifesting more clearly the person you can be and are meant to be. That calls for a continual reshaping of your vision for your life together in the first domain.

I have a friend who convinced her husband to buy a sailboat. They were all excited about it. They could afford it, they both loved being around the ocean, they had weekends to burn – everything seemed just right. They were careful in selecting the right boat and the right place to park it.

We kind of lost track of each other for several years but then one weekend I ran into her at a weekend coaching workshop. I asked about the boat before I asked about them because I had been so taken with the romance of it all.

She said, "The boat? Oh, the sailboat." Then she started to laugh. Short version of the story was this: they got pregnant three months after purchasing the boat and it became too much of a hassle for them to spend much time on it. Besides, they now needed the money they were spending on the note and maintenance.

More important, the joy of home time replaced the joy of time out on the ocean. They decided they needed to invest in a larger home. Their vision for their life together changed in a very short time. Will it change again? I hope so, because that's what is supposed to happen.

To manifest your love in this relationship at this time means you'll have to fully accept the right you have been given to be the individual you are. There's no room for orphan psychology. No room for whining, competing, or withdrawing. You'll have to step into your own shoes and stand in them.

And you'll both need to invite the other into the reshaping of your vision. That is the essence of manifesting your love within the domain of roommates.

D. OWNING YOUR OWN WORK – THE INNER JOURNEY

What does a person who owns their own inner work look like? Here are a few indicators important in your efforts to withdraw analysis of, and projections onto, your partner.

When you own your own inner work:

- you are no longer combative
- you develop the capacity to slow way down under pressure
- you don't blame others for the unhappiness you feel
- you lose your angry mood
- you are emotionally sober
- you ask rather than tell your partner what they are feeling
- humility is your companion
- your authority is clear and open
- your love flows

There are others, but these should start the conversation.

E. INDIVIDUATION AND INTIMACY – THE JOURNEY INTO INTIMACY

There is a strange polarity between the need for individuation and the need for intimacy. Many of us do not know how to be all that we are and still be intimate without compromising ourselves. I relate this to the challenge of becoming legitimate.

The temptation to compromise the essence of who you are in order to gain favor with your love is a big one. It is also misleading. Many voices will whisper in your ear: "you better not say that, you'll upset him," or "She meant well," or "Why bring it up now" or "we can't say everything we think all the time, can we?" (I like this one because it's so seductive. Of course we can't say everything we think all the time, there's not enough time to do that. But we can say what's *emotionally relevant* all the time at the time it is relevant).

Compromise isn't the same as sensitivity to your partner. You'll have to know the difference. If you don't, get some help because it's an extremely important distinction. Compromise is learned. It's strategic. It's fear based. It's an anti-relational tactic that makes the compromiser look good to him/herself.

The truth is this. The best gift you can give to your partner is the kindest and clearest expression of who you are at all times. It opens the way to intimacy because true intimacy is based on real openness, honesty, loving communication, and the embrace of conflict. Avoidance is self protection, and self protection is an attempt to not expose how you love, your truth, your engagement. Avoidance is a false attempt at safety.

F. FILTERS

Just a word about filters. Loving requires two things here. One is that you become familiar with the filters you use, and the other is that you question their value. Earlier we looked at the role parents play in distorting our ability to love. Our parents had their filters, we have ours. My mom thought discussion about sexuality was inappropriate. My dad believed his angry feelings were bad for his family. These filtered out much good, needed conversation in our family.

I "saw" that they filtered these conversations out, but I didn't realize I was contaminated with the same filters. Much of psychotherapy centers on the drama of this kind of discovery.

When I started to awaken to my own filters – some religion based, some parental, some based on painful experiences with teachers, professors, or friends – the awakening caused no small amount of grief.

Filtering limits the expression not only of what's "off limits," it also snags great pieces of our loving.

Like gill nets in the ocean that not only catch the targeted fish but many other species, filtering severely limits the free flow of our natural, loving energies. Pay attention to your filters, confront them, and remove them one-by-one.

PART XI

SOME OTHER THINGS TO REMEMBER

A. IT'S A MARATHON, NOT A SPRINT

Loving each other and creating a sustainable vision in which you both continuously experience enthusiasm for intimacy, relationship, and partnering is a lifelong adventure.

That's one reason for "till death us do part." It takes time. Marriage is meant to be a container for the careful and often slow unveiling of both your individual potential and the potential in your relationship.

In our workshops there is often great enthusiasm for the possibilities that working with the three journeys provokes. Some couples will tell us that their lives have changed when using these ideas in their relationship. We are happy for them and happy to be part of that shift in consciousness. We also remind them that it's a beginning.

It's a marathon, not a sprint. Marriage is meant to be a total life experience. Too much enthusiasm too quickly deceives us into thinking we're done. Learn to slow down and accept each insight, each new idea, as a piece of the ongoing challenge, and realize as fully as possible the capabilities and capacities of your love.

B. THE CHALLENGE OF NAVIGATION

Moving among the three journeys takes practice and patience. The idea here is to play with the notion of what journey you are primarily in. Let yourself be conscious of it, and when you can, identify journeys with each other. Do it out loud. You'll be surprised at what happens to communication challenges when you do.

Knowing where you are helps you navigate within that journey. If I'm in the Inner Journey, reflecting on my dreams, evaluating my parents marriage and its influence on what I expect or what I filter out, focusing on the quality of my own masculinity or re-working some old wounds, then I will not be very available to my partner's need to discuss buying a new couch.

If I know where I am, I can do two things. I can communicate that to her and she'll give me space to stay there as long as I need to, and I can honor my own work with attentiveness and focus. I will not be so likely to jump around from domain to domain.

C. THE ART OF TRANSITION

Moving from one domain to another often occurs naturally, but just as often requires conscious attention. A simple trick is to make the transition conscious. Like this: "I am deep into some personal stuff right now and so I don't have much interest in the couch. I'd like to get to that with you, though. Can we talk about it after dinner?"

Or, "I'm excited about a new couch I saw today. Are you available to talk about it with me?" Or, "When would be a good time to talk about it?" These are simple invitations to transition. They are kind and respectful of your partner. They acknowledge that we often are tripping along in our own journey whether that be roommate stuff, inner work, or contemplating an intimate conversation.

The necessity is to be conscious of the need for transition even though at first it may seem artificial and/ or awkward. Following the transition you will feel the ease of knowing where you are and what you're doing there without worrying about where your partner is. As we said, "life works, when we keep our agreements."

D. EXPANDING YOUR OWN PARADIGM

We are suggesting that all of us challenge the paradigm of marriage that we live within. In this book we introduced you to the three journeys. Paradigms are meant to expand, change, and be replaced with more relevant, nourishing.

and true ideas. Allow room for expansion of your paradigm and share it with us. We'll share your ideas through our website, podcasts and coaching with other couples.

In the second book we'll offer some ideas on creating your own philosophy of marriage, tending your garden, and some competencies that may help you realize the marriage you dream you would like to have.

PART XII

CONCLUSION

We've introduced you to the three journeys in marriage. Our simple observations have opened conversations, clarified conflict, and deepened intimacy in our own relationship. We've become better at loving one another, more empathic, and certainly less inclined to give up on each other.

Exploring the domains, rings, and journeys has helped us expose our naiveté in some areas (money and personal authority come to mind) and our hunger in others - the desire to surrender and claim the promises of our bodies. Domain awareness helps us to talk more clearly and respect each other. We marvel at our growth as we experience and work with the seven principles. And we continually work to consciously tend the roots of our love.

We are more open these days, inviting friends into the marriage conversation. Our workshops have magically become less structured and more powerful, though there's still plenty of structure. A growing community of couples support, share, mentor, and enjoy one another as we embrace together our commitment to healthy marriages.

We see changes in our children as well. Embracing conflict reduces arguments and at the same time clarifies the natural differences individuals must work with in order to live together. Children learn that their conflicts are legitimate and that, coupled with domain consciousness, pretty much eliminates whining, complaining, and moodiness. Children experience their legitimate place within the family and the legitimacy of their needs and gifts.

We want our children and grandchildren to grow their own personal authority, share their spiritual insights, and fully express the considerable range of their emotions. They are a vital part of the health of this family.

Awareness is not only an individual process but is dependent on the micro-community we live in. We look for opportunities to energetically share our journeys, challenge accepted realities, and celebrate our love.

Notice that the kinds of self talk that is laced with judgment of others, diagnosis and analysis, theories, speculations, and projections are a brain killer. Judgment is a fear-based response to change or differences. If you are willing to take the 100% rule seriously and own your awareness of discomfort, then judgment evaporates.

Marriage, like deep friendship, needs transformation and it needs renewal. In talking about marriage, the poet Wendell Berry said, "It is to be broken, it is never whole..." This is the way of relationship evolution.

One morning not long ago our five-year-old daughter asked to take out her white "flower girl" dress, the one she wore to her brother's wedding. Her mother said "Sure, why not."

I said "Be careful," thinking of the $30 cleaning bill we paid readying it for storage.

She, ever living in the exact center of her personal authority, said: "I'll be careful. I want to try it on."

Sitting in the middle of the living room floor, white satin spread around her in a circle, face beaming, she said, "I'm going to marry Caden."

We know the longing and we recognize the deep desire to mate and share ourselves. In this sharing you will know life more fully than is possible any other way. My wife and I looked at each other, "Yes, but not yet."

PART XIII

LOOKING AHEAD

Challenging the paradigm you live within, becoming comfortable with new language for communication, learning to embrace conflict, creating building blocks for transforming your marriage and more – all can be a lot of fun. It can be painful, frustrating and sometimes frightening as well. We are not polyannas about marriage.

The good news is your marriage awaits your closer attentiveness. And the rewards of focusing on rebirthing your own marriage are tremendous. In Volume II we'll offer some competencies and skills that will help. Here's a look ahead.

A. COMPETENCIES

1. In Book II we'll take a look at the role of **Natural Genius** in relationship. Most of us are fairly clueless about the gold we bring to relationship. Our Gift, or Natural Genius, is assumed and usually we overlook or aren't aware of that critical dynamic, its sweetness, its brilliance, and its relevance to many challenges we face.

2. **Self-esteem**. We'll offer a simple model for moving through beginning awareness of what's going on to resolving and including your awareness in the quality of your relationship. This process is one that increases self-esteem and gives you reason to stand up for your own presence and your own love.

3. **Listening**. We've identified three listening styles that capture the demands and challenges of life as partners in marriage. From "resonant listening" to "active listening" we'll look at how an awareness of each situation can drive an awareness of a listening competency that's muscular and relevant to where you're trying to go and what you're trying to accomplish. Domains will shape the listening style you choose, but so will time, interest, and need.

4. **Conflict.** We haven't given you much yet on the importance of embracing conflict but we will. I have noticed in my years of experience that whether I am dealing with an executive team or a married couple, this competency is in need of attention.

   We'll relate the embrace of conflict to trust building, communication that works, and accountability with a clear model of success. Conflict embraced becomes a major pathway to intimacy and deep friendship.

6. **Entheos.** The idea that we have within us the capacity for a relationship in which we can experience enthusiasm for that relationship over the life of the relationship is astounding. Sustainable enthusiasm is an achievable goal. In fact, we are promised at birth that such is possible.

We are conceived within the love of two parents. We are born believing in the sustainability of their love for each other and their love for us. The fact that many of our parents weren't able to realize the promise of their love does not cancel out the promise. I believe that deep within each of us that promise lives and it is our task to realize it.

Not only that, but our children have the right to expect our fullest energies and commitment to the realization of that promise. The work of creating the *With These Rings* model of marriage is based on that belief.

B. TWO OTHER FOUNDATIONS OF HEALTHY MARRIAGE

We'll look at the idea of creating a working philosophy of marriage based on

Seven Principles we use to inform our own work in our marriage. These need-based principles will help you build a structure for your marriage that holds all the challenges you face in a believable context.

Additionally, we'll look at the genesis of your love. We call it "tending the roots" of the garden that is your love home. We'll offer pathways to re-connecting to your love, competencies for vitalizing it in your life today, and images that help you sustain its core.

All this could be summarized in a re-statement of vows. We'll revisit your vows and nuptials and offer some guidelines for creating vows that reflect your current philosophy of marriage.

If this first book succeeds in any way to introduce you to a fresh way to re-imagine your marriage, the second book will offer tools, skill sets, and competencies for realizing the marriage that you dream is possible.

It is.

..."the woods are lovely, dark and deep
but I have promises to keep
and miles to go before I sleep
miles to go before I sleep."

- Robert Frost, "Stopping by Woods on a Snowy Evening"

THE AUTHOR

STEPHEN W. FRUEH consults and coaches business leaders and corporate teams by assessing and impacting leadership effectiveness. He coaches couples on creating new approaches to "The Marriage Conversation," helping them to revitalize and renew their relationship.

These two dimensions of his work in many ways mirror each other: the leadership conversations contain personal factors that, when addressed, significantly expand an executive's impact and effectiveness; similarly, many couples are finding that carefully studying their personal paradigms opens a pathway to new energy, greater intimacy, clearer conversations, and increased relational competencies.

Stephen offers workshops with his wife Lynn – a marriage and family therapist – on a number of dimensions within the marriage conversation. They invite couples into a new way of thinking about marriage, one that sustains enthusiasm for the relationship and supports a life-long commitment.

Stephen is available as a keynote speaker. He is a member of the National Speakers Association and is an engaging workshop and seminar leader.

Stephen offers coaching and consulting services to businesses and couples who seek to more fully realize their potentials.

You can contact Stephen at **805 527 2600** (WTR) or **805 338 4286** or email him **Stephen@withtheserings.com**

www.ingramcontent.com/pod-product-compliance
Lightning Source LLC
LaVergne TN
LVHW020642100826
845148LV00012B/2302

* 9 7 8 1 5 9 9 3 2 0 3 8 0 *